Sexual Misconduct and the Future of Mega-Churches

Sexual Misconduct and the Future of Mega-Churches

How Large Religious Organizations Go Astray

Glenn L. Starks

PRAEGER

AN IMPRINT OF ABC-CLIO, LLC
Santa Barbara, California • Denver, Colorado • Oxford, England

Copyright 2013 by ABC-CLIO, LLC

All rights reserved. No part of this publication may be reproduced, stored in a retrieval system, or transmitted, in any form or by any means, electronic, mechanical, photocopying, recording, or otherwise, except for the inclusion of brief quotations in a review, without prior permission in writing from the publisher.

Library of Congress Cataloging-in-Publication Data

Starks, Glenn L., 1966–
  Sexual misconduct and the future of mega-churches : how large religious organizations go astray / Glenn L. Starks.
    p. cm.
  Includes bibliographical references and index.
    ISBN 978–1–4408–0391–8 (cloth : alk. paper) — ISBN 978–1–4408–0392–5 (ebook)
  1. Sexual misconduct by clergy. 2. Clergy—Sexual behavior. 3. Big churches. I. Title.
  BV4392.5.S73 2013
  261.8′3272—dc23   2012039006

ISBN: 978–1–4408–0391–8
EISBN: 978–1–4408–0392–5

17 16 15 14 13   1 2 3 4 5

This book is also available on the World Wide Web as an eBook.
Visit www.abc-clio.com for details.

Praeger
An Imprint of ABC-CLIO, LLC

ABC-CLIO, LLC
130 Cremona Drive, P.O. Box 1911
Santa Barbara, California 93116-1911

This book is printed on acid-free paper ∞

Manufactured in the United States of America

Contents

Introduction	vii
Chapter 1. Profile of Mega-Churches	1
Chapter 2. Mega-Church Leaders: Sex over Faith and Accountability?	17
Chapter 3. No Crimes Are Victimless: Who Are Mega-Church Leaders Committing Sexual Misconduct With?	59
Chapter 4. The Silence of the Church: Is it Supporting the Minister in His Sexual Misdeeds?	79
Chapter 5. Implications for Society: Bad Actions Breed Discontent	99
Chapter 6. How to End the Suffering: Strategies to End Sexual Misconduct in Mega-Churches	111
Chapter 7. Conclusion: The Future of Mega-Churches in a Climate of Sexual Corruption	125
Appendix: Top 10 Mega-Churches in America	133
Notes	135
Bibliography	145
Index	153

Introduction

Mega-churches are the most recent phenomenon in American religion. These churches have revolutionized religion by combining religious theology with secular methods of entertainment. To electrify attendees and motivate members, dynamic sermons, music, dancers, state-of-the-art lighting systems, and stadium-size seating have replaced stodgy theology-based sermons, choirs singing from hymnals, and conventional church pews. Mega-church leaders have gained so much influence that they are able to grow their church memberships into thousands of devout worshippers. These charismatic showmen (99% of mega-church leaders are men) spread their messages around the world using satellite campuses, television, the Internet, and best-selling books and compact discs. They are advisors to presidents and movie producers, and live lavish lifestyles comparable to those of rock stars. Millions of people love them, crediting them with bringing throngs of nonworshippers back into the church, but equally millions criticize them for secularizing religion in order to grow their multi-million dollar churches.

Many consider mega-churches a religious and cultural fad. They gained prominence in the 1970s due to a social and cultural shift in the United States characterized by a distrust of bureaucratic organized entities, including the government and organized religions. In 1970, there were only 10 fully established mega-churches in the United States. By 2011, there were approximately 1,200. Significant problems accompanied their growth, including accusations that ministers were embezzling millions of dollars. While many mega-churches hid behind their tax-exempt status, many of their ministers were living in mansions, traveling in private jets, and driving luxury cars. Some even began using their positions to influence local, state, and national politics.

Yet one issue over all others has dominated the criticism of mega-churches: widespread instances of mega-church leaders committing acts of sexual misconduct. Over the past few decades, numerous mega-church ministers have been alleged to have sexually abused children, or have been convicted of such. In addition, they have been accused and sometimes convicted of obtaining the sexual services of prostitutes, molesting church members during religious ceremonies, and manipulating church members into having extramarital affairs. These incidents have been so shocking in their details that they have made front-page news and been the feature of television news programs. Ministers like Jimmy Swaggart, Eddie Long, Ted Haggard, Earl Paulk, and Zachary Tims have created a national debate over why such powerful individuals who were trusted by many could have committed such acts. Furthermore, how could men who professed to be so religiously devout have committed moral failings that are contrary to the basic foundations of their theologies and religion in general? Theirs and the actions of so many other ministers have so outraged the nation that they are now negatively impacting the perception of religion in general, much as the incidents of sexual abuse by priests in the Roman Catholic Church have affected its reputation. As the number of mega-churches grows, the number of incidents is also growing and getting more bizarre. There are now mega-church ministers who are convicted child molesters, fathers of illegitimate children, and parolees due to having multiple trysts with prostitutes. Ministers that embezzle millions of dollars, place family members and sexual partners on the church payroll, and use church funds to purchase expensive cars and mansions have created a negative view of mega-churches.

This book will explore the various factors—direct and indirect situational, psychological, demographic, and social—leading individuals who were chosen to lead so many to risk the trust of their followers for personal gratification and to break the very commandments they have dedicated their lives to teach others.

This book uses a combination of theoretical discussion, references to relevant articles and studies, and details of actual events to fully shape a review of this issue. To frame a context for this discussion, Chapter 1 provides a thorough summary of the history and current status of mega-churches in order to provide a framework of their religious scope and purpose. Chapter 2 analyzes the reasons mega-church leaders commit acts of sexual misconduct. Included is an exploration of psychological, demographic, and economic theories as to why these acts take place, along with examples based on actual incidents. The purpose of this chapter is to outline the innate reasons for misconduct within the psyche of the perpetrator. Chapter 3 explores the various ways victims react to perpetrators' behavior. These acts include remaining silent after a first encounter out of fear, remaining silent due to self-esteem issues, or accepting financial or other compensation in exchange for sex. This chapter does not seek to support the acts of the perpetrators; rather, it discusses how circumstances can support the continuation of some incidents. Chapter 4 discusses the silence of the church when mega-church ministers commit acts of sexual misconduct. There is evidence that the members of mega-churches support their church leaders even when there is overwhelming evidence of their guilt by virtue of the leaders' power and/or position, dismissing the acts of church leaders on the basis of forgiveness, or condemning a secular spotlight on what is deemed an internal church matter. This chapter explores these and other factors that contribute to perpetrator behavior by the actions or lack thereof by religious organizations and church congregations.

Chapter 5 explores the implications of these incidents on society. Because of numerous cases of misconduct by leaders of some of the nation's most prominent mega-churches, many people have a negative view of these large churches and their trust in single leader who has gained so much power. This chapter explores society's attitudes in terms of their faith in and attitudes toward mega-churches, the impact on their religious and spiritual viewpoints, and their general trust in religious leaders and religion itself. Chapter 6 discusses recommendations to stop acts of misconduct by leaders of mega-churches by using strategies to curb or prevent these incidents from occurring again. The basis of discussion is the reasons these incidents occur, as discussed in the first three chapters, as well as recommendations related to what can be done by churches, religious organizations, law enforcement agencies, community groups, and welfare networks. Finally, Chapter 7 discusses the future of mega-churches. Can mega-churches continue to place such large responsibility and power in the hands of one person or a small group? What changes might be necessary for these organizations to be able to continue serving the needs of their large congregations? Such are the issues confronting the U.S. mega-church in the 21st century.

Chapter 1

Profile of Mega-Churches

Mega-churches are a relatively recent phenomenon in American religion, a phenomenon that began in the 1950s, expanded in the 1970s, and experienced a membership explosion during the 1980s and 1990s. The relatively sudden growth of so many of these of these churches led to what some call the mega-church movement. Called seeker churches, mega-churches target young members and those who have never or no longer attend any type of church (or the "unchurched") through a secular-based approach to worship. These churches also increase membership by attracting members from smaller churches that cannot compete with the glitz, variety of programs, and dynamic yet charismatic ministers of mega-churches.

They are also called new-age or re-envisioned churches because their worship style relies less on formal religious worship based on theology and more on entertainment through music and visual effects. As Jorstad summarizes in *Popular Religion in America: The Evangelical Voice*, mega-churches are so popular for six reasons: "high-powered celebrity preachers, TV-style worship, reliance on drama, popular music, and secular music instrumentation." He further states that these churches have "an image of anonymity that mirrors mass society because some seekers feel uncomfortable in small-group settings; a wide variety of ministries, especially mass media items; and a willingness to change rapidly with the shifting whims of the marketplace, quickly dropping or adding programs according to congregational interests."[1] These and other characteristics will be discussed further later in this chapter.

2 Sexual Misconduct and the Future of Mega-Churches

In 1970, there were only 10 fully established mega-churches in the United States. By 2011, there were approximately 1,200 with combined annual revenues of over $7 billion. Between 2000 and 2005, the average attendance at mega-churches grew 57 percent, from 2,279 to 3,585.[2] If all of these churches were combined under one religion, they would collectively represent the third largest denomination in the United States behind Roman Catholic and Baptist.

Mega-churches evolved as other religious movements did: through a shift in religious thinking. As stated by Loveland and Wheeler in *From Meetinghouse to Megachurch: A Material and Cultural History*, "Just as the Puritans developed a 'new architectural creation' to reflect their religious beliefs and worship practices, the revivalists of the Second Great Awakening introduced new structures for religious gatherings that helped them accomplish their main objective–converting sinners to Protestant Christianity and persuading them to become church members. Their structures constituted an important link in the evolution of the late twentieth-century mega-churches because they incorporated evangelistic strategies used by later generations of evangelicals, including those associated with mega-churches."[3]

As part of the cultural and social shift toward secularism that occurred in the United States beginning in the 1970s, these churches expanded as "spirituality" gained greater prominence. Spirituality is the embodiment of being personally connected with a higher reality of existence through a communal connection with humanity, nature, and the universe. It also encompasses a belief in a greater power or consciousness that is communed with through prayer and other methods of spiritual communication. Each individual thus has the ability to personally connect with this higher power, particularly to find guidance, purpose, and the meaning of life. This shift in religious thinking greatly impacted organized and traditional religion. As Douthat discussed in *Bad Religion: How We Became a Nation of Heretics*,

the crisis of traditional Christianity, not the rise of the conservative churches, remains the major religious story of the 1960s and 70s. The gains of certain denominations notwithstanding, the era witnessed an extraordinary weakening of organized Christianity in the United States and a fundamental shift in America's spiritual ecology—away from institutional religion and toward a more do-it-yourself and consumer-oriented spirituality—that endures to the present day. In subsequent decades, traditional believers would hopefully cite various revivals or awakenings as evidence that faith might be regaining the ground it lost between 1965 and 1980. But nothing that's happened since, whether in small prayer groups or booming mega-churches, has made up for the losses that institutional Christianity sustained during America's cultural revolution.[4]

In general during this time period, there grew a distrust of bureaucratic organized entities, including the government and organized religions such as the Roman Catholic Church. They were viewed as entities that attempted to control people through strict dogma and a hierarchical structure in which the many answered to a powerful few. Those in power spoke on behalf of followers, whether in setting laws or dictating the proper and moral behavior in an individual's life. In order words, there was no individual voice. The theology of the church was stolid, and the individual's role was to adapt, regardless of personal feelings or trends reshaping society or culture. However, this was in conflict with a growing need for individualism in society. In his book *The Megachurch and the Mainline: Remaking Religious Tradition in the Twenty-first Century,* Ellingson wrote on the causes and results of changes in general religious practice and philosophy in a society. He explained that

the catalyst for changes in religious ideas, practices, or structures comes from external sources, often depicted as a crisis that a congregation or religious organization must address in order to survive. In Wuthnow's account, some disturbance to the moral order leads to the production of new ideologies. In an uncertain environment, creators compete with one another for resources or potential followers as they attempt to adapt to the emergent environment. As in Weber's model, the winners of this competition gain support for their ideology because it resonates more closely with the needs or interests of target audiences than other ideologies. The change process concludes when the new ideology is institutionalized and a new moral order is established.[5]

Ellingson references the writings of Dr. Robert Wuthnow, an American writer and sociologist of religion, culture, and civil society. Wuthnow explained moral order as being determined by social customs and conventions that serve to maintain social order. In this context, a disturbance to the moral order such as a major shift in religious ideological thinking and behavior leads to new leaders. The disturbance that occurred during in the 1970s was a deprivation of individual needs being met through hierarchical religions. Mega-churches thus arose as a method to fill this deprivation through the opportunity created by the disturbance. Ellingson also references the work of German sociologist, political economist, and philosopher Max Weber. Weber believed religion shapes an individual's view of the world. Religious organizations will thus change their religious ethics (or theologies) to be in congruence with the belief structures of individuals. In the case of mega-churches, this change was the embracing of nondenominational theologies in order to be in congruence with the individualistic spiritual theologies of individuals. Other churches that did not at least attempt to adapt to the changing needs and desires of its members often lost them.

The combination of distrust of organized religions, individual desire to worship as one wanted, and an embracing of secular life were the catalysts for transforming American religion. The nondenomination of many mega-churches was part of the community church movement in which Protestants and evangelicals sought ecumenism, or the desire to worship as Christians but not under a religious denomination. As explained by Turner in *The New Blackwell Companion to the Sociology of Religion,*

First, mega-churches reflect the continued growth of evangelicalism in terms of numbers and market share. Second, mega-churches may be reshaping the denominational system in the United States both by intensifying the push towards non-denominationalism and by creating new, decentralized quasi-denominations that may take on some of the functions of older denominations without the costs or negative image of the older, hierarchical denominational bodies. Third, they may be redefining Protestant religious culture as increasing numbers of congregations, across denominations adopt the worship practices, educational materials, and theological ideas employed by successful mega-churches.[6]

As further explained by Bilrzikian and Ortberg in *Community 101: Reclaiming the Local Church as Community of Oneness,* "An increasing number of Christians are waking up to the fact that, to a large extent, the church has become ineffective in fulfilling its mission because it has lost a sense of its own identify as community. They realize that not every organization that calls itself a church represents the church as Christ conceived it. As a result, we observe, toward the end of the second millennium of the life of the church, the emergence of a 'community movement.'"[7]

Although mega-churches have been described as a recent phenomenon in American culture, large churches in global religious history are not new. Large Roman Catholic cathedrals, Islamic mosques, and Protestant churches are examples that have individually served hundreds or thousands of members. Mega-churches borrow from their use of aesthetics to attract members. As Loveland and Wheeler point out in *From Meetinghouse to Megachurch,* "The earliest American antecedent of the late-twentieth century evangelical mega-churches was the seventeenth-century and early eighteenth-century meetinghouse, the 'new architectural creation' devised by the English Puritans who settled Massachusetts Bay in 1630. Their main contribution to the evolution of the mega-churches was a functionalist aesthetic that mandated designing religious buildings to suit the purposes, beliefs, and activities of the people who used them."[8]

American mega-churches are unique, however, due to the nature of religion in the United States. First, the United States is the most religiously diverse nation in the world due to a mix of so many different cultures, races, and ethnic groups. Religions in other many countries are relatively homogenous. Mega-churches provide forums of worship that serve the religious needs of their members, regardless of their past affiliation to any particular denomination or religious sect. Second, the United States was founded based on the premise of religious freedom. Religious persecution in Europe was one of the primary factors that led to the nation's founding. The separation of church and state so basic to the U.S. Constitution has ensured the government cannot require individuals to practice any particular religion or even that they must practice religion at all. Therefore, religious practice in the United States is based on an individual's desire and personal connection to a religious body. This has created a nation of strong religious beliefs because of guaranteed individual freedom of choice. Last, the United States is the most religious nation in comparison to other nations of comparable wealth. Being a rich nation that is based on the premise of capitalism, religion has become a competitive commodity. As Kohut and Stokes discuss in *America against the World*, "By almost every measure, the United States is the most religious rich nation in the world. Indeed, it is the only religious rich nation in the world ... Americans are more religious than other wealthy, educated peoples because they live in a more open religious market, with more churches and greater variety of religious perspectives competing for their devotion. With more options, Americans have blossomed into great consumers of religion. Secular Europeans, in contrast, live in an uncompetitive market."[9]

Much of the decision making done by Americans in choosing products offered in a commercial market are based on entertainment. Choice is driven by how products are marketed using audio and visual effects in a way to speak to their beliefs, needs, and desires. This begins when people are children and continues through their entire lives. It begins with a colorful clown used to promote hamburgers, then flashy music videos to sell cars, a circus-like environment that drives where people shop, and continues with the use of a retired but famous movie star to convince seniors what insurance to buy. Companies continually develop new and creative advertisements to entire buyers. Those who do not find themselves pushed out of the market by others who can better attract buyers. Mega-churches and other religious entities have resorted to the same strategies. They compete with one another but also with entities that seek to persuade consumers to spend their leisure time with them (e.g., shopping centers, amusement parks, and sporting venues). Consider the following points raised by White and Yeats in *Franchising McChurch:*

6   Sexual Misconduct and the Future of Mega-Churches

Feeding Our Obsession with Easy Christianity on how American religion has become a marketplace, or what they define as a Buffet of Religion:

> Think of countless children's ministries across the United States. Destined to be the future leaders of the church, what has been the steady diet of many of these young adults? Entertainment. Most children's Sunday schools quit reading and studying the Bible long ago. Instead, children view cartoon adaptations of the text along with numerous activities that keep them entertained while Mom and Dad worship without distraction. Moving to youth groups, many of these same kids rely on emotional experiences, graphical images, game times, and vacuous messages. The churches that have the largest population of students are frequently those that provide the best entertainment for kids. In many towns, the religiously oriented youth, savvy shoppers that they are, simply attend the church that has the greatest concentration of entertaining events.
>
> Assuming these young adults stay in church (which is the last thing we should assume given the statistics), what do we assume their expectations for church services will be? Society has trained them to be careful consumers, with an uncanny ability to ferret out what best suits their personal desires. Christianity, for many in American culture, is simply a selection on the Buffet of Religion. If they buy into Christianity through entertainment, the show must go on to keep them engaged. Thanks to the law of diminishing returns, that same show must continue to attract their attention with newer or greater thing, or else these shoppers will find another, more interesting show down the road, which may or may not be another church.[10]

Mega-churches are defined as churches with weekly attendance of at least 2,000 persons per week. Some have congregations of over 40,000 members. Table 1.1 shows the distribution of mega-churches by number of weekly attendees. (Also see the appendix, "Top 10 Mega-Churches in America" for details on the largest mega-churches in the United States.) Mega-churches with the largest memberships are called gigachurches and are defined as churches with weekly attendance of 10,000 or more. For example, Joel Osteen's Lakewood Church in Houston, Texas, has a membership of 43,500 and is housed in downtown Houston's Compaq Center, the 16,500-seat former arena of the Houston Rockets. The church spent $95 million to renovate the arena and pays $12.1 million in rent to the City of Houston (for 30 years, starting in 2004 when it first leased the site, with an option to extend the lease for an additional 30 years for $22.6 million).[11] Services are broadcast on television in the United States and approximately 100 other countries. In 2012, it was the largest mega-church in the United States. Its annual operating budget is between $70 million and $1 billion. Hundreds line up to greet Osteen as well as his wife and copastor, Victoria, after each service.

Table 1.1
Mega-Church Distribution by Size

Number of Attendees	Percentage of Mega-Churches
2,000–2,999	53.8
3,000–3,999	19.1
4,000–4,999	11.1
5,000–9,999	12.0
10,000 or more	4.0

Source: Thumma, Scott and Travis, Dave. *Beyond Megachurch Myths: What We Can Learn from America's Largest Churches* (San Francisco, CA: John Wiley & Sons, 2007).

Just as a note, mega-churches are not only a U.S. phenomenon. They are located in other countries, particularly in Asia. The largest mega-churches in the world are located in southern Asia, Africa, and South America. In fact, the largest mega-church in the world is located in Seoul, South Korea, on Yoido Island. Yoido Full Gospel Church is a Pentecostal church founded and led by David Yonggi Cho. He and his mother-in-law (also a minister) founded the church in his home in 1958. The church now professes to have nearly 1 million members. The church is so large that its seven Sunday services are translated into 16 languages and broadcast on television. Just as with U.S. mega-churches, many of those around the world are also battling scandals dealing with sexual misconduct by their ministers.

Even with their large sizes, mega-churches do not represent the majority of all churches in terms of having the majority of attendees. The majority of Americans attend churches with 200 or fewer members. However, mega-churches have had the greatest influence on U.S. religion since the 1970s. As discussed in the article "The Trend toward Bigger Churches: Going Mega" by Dart,

The estimated 1,350 mega-churches in the country amount to less than 0.5 percent of the 300,000 congregations in the United States, but they reach a wide swath of people and in some ways set the tone for much of the Protestant world. "On any given weekend, 9 percent of churchgoers attend a mega-church," said sociologist Warren Bird, research director for the evangelically oriented Leadership Network. The attendance gap between mega-churches and most Protestant churches is striking. The median U.S. church has 75 regular participants in worship on Sundays. Only 5 percent of the nation's churches have an average of more than 500 churchgoers on a weekend.[12]

Most mega-churches are Protestant Christian and theological evangelical in practice, which means these churches practice faith according to the Bible and believe it is based on the guidance of or writings directed by God. Evangelists include Southern Baptists, Lutherans, and Methodists. Approximately one-third of mega-churches are nondenominational or multidenominational. Nondenominational churches include those that have never supported nor conducted services geared toward a specific religion and those that once identified themselves with a specific religion such as Catholicism. As evangelist churches, their leaders and members espouse a devotion to spirituality or a higher power, and denounce what they consider objectionable moral behavior such as abortion, fornication, adultery, infidelity, and homosexuality. Other activities considered mortal sins include stealing, lying, and jealousy. Due to their large memberships, and their leaders having best-selling publications, worldwide Internet coverage, and local and national influence with government leaders, they impact smaller churches as well as other ministers and pastors around the world.

Mega-churches share other similar characteristics. They conduct their missions and increase their membership numbers in the same way as profitable private businesses. They are consumerist in nature rather than theology based in that they conduct market surveys to both satisfy the needs of current members and to increase their numbers of new customers. Seeking new members is part of the church's religious purpose, but the practice also serves to increase its financial solidity. Mega-churches are called seeker churches because they target people who are new to the Christian faith. Often they evolve from nonexistent or modest churches to mega-churches in the course of one to five years because of aggressive advertising to increase their memberships. Their rapid growth often causes controversy within their communities, which leads to increased membership out of spectator curiosity. Most were started by a single person serving as the church's religious leader and a small congregation of people. For example, Bishop T. D. Jakes, pastor of the Potter's House in Dallas, Texas, began his first church in Montgomery, West Virginia, with 10 members. In 2012, the Potter's House had 30,000 members. Church sermons are broadcast around the world on several television networks. The church also has additional campuses in North Dallas and Fort Worth, Texas, and in Denver, Colorado.

Mega-churches are initially founded in places such as small churches, basements, living rooms, and community centers. As they grow, they move into school auditoriums, circus tents, and abandoned shopping centers. They eventually build large churches or lease or purchase buildings as large as stadiums. As they continue to grow, they expand their current structures, expand into campuses, and/or expand with satellite locations. For example, Community Christian Church is headquartered in Naperville, Illinois, and had churches in 10 other cities throughout

Illinois as of 2012. Seacoast Church is headquartered in Mount Pleasant, South Carolina. It has campuses in eight locations in South Carolina, two in North Carolina, and one in Georgia. The church's slogan on its website is "One Church. Many Campuses."

Mega-church ministers and their senior staffs engage in clever tactics to attract new members, much like the presidents of corporations. In *Shopping for God: How Christianity Went from In Your Heart to In Your Face*, James Twitchell describes mega-church leaders as "pastorpreneurs" who "by clever use of marketing techniques . . . have been able to create what are essentially city-states of believers."[13] He further aptly compares mega-churches to shopping malls in terms of size and marketing. He states,

The mall store is not at all that far from the mega-church. The big mega-churches look eerily alike, a slightly different version of Safeway. A number of observers have pointed to the often provocative similarities between the medieval cathedral and the modern department store: both are concerned with salvation via consumption, getting the Word out (proselytizing/advertising), and ranks of affiliation (devotion/brand loyalty). Furthermore, both have sacred tests (Bible/catalog), functionaries (clergy/clerks), signs of spiritual election (salvation/goods), holidays (religious/sales), heroic lighting (stained glass/spotlights), music (hymns/Muzak), and financial transactions (tithe/purchase and collection plate/cash register).[14]

In *Religion: From Their Origins to the Twenty-first Century*, Peter Williams wrote about how mega-churches evolved from a marketing movement:

Mega-churches did not just happen, but emerged through marketing research, based on secular business practices, and modeled and aimed at the continually expanding exurban population of newly moved, upwardly mobile, and religiously uprooted Americans who now constituted a major new demographic category. Externally, these buildings often avoid the traditional trappings of Christian houses of worship, such as steeples and crosses, and more closely resemble secular structures such as conference hotels or shopping malls. Names, such as "Christian Life Center" are also frequently nontraditional, reflecting the Reformed tradition's rejection of the notion of sacred space while simultaneously appealing to the sensibilities of the secularized suburbanite. The worship spaces themselves echo the "auditorium churches" of the late nineteenth century in their focus on preaching and music rather than elaborate liturgy. Arrays of musical instruments are often found on the stages, together with state-of-the art technological systems of amplification and projection. The old-time gospel songs have in many cases yielded to the new style "praise songs," musically uncomplicated pieces influenced by contemporary secular styles; similarly the organ has given place to the electronic keyboard or electric guitar.[15]

As stated earlier, many mega-churches are so large and their memberships so dispersed that sermons are broadcast on the Internet or on television and radio, or they are published on CDs and video, and in book form. Many hold two or three services on Sundays to accommodate all of their local members. To provide a broad range of services, the primary ministers have assistant ministers who are each assigned to lead a specific segment of the church service. For example, there may be a minister of music in charge of the various choirs and bands. The pastor of the children's ministry leads youth Bible study, baptisms, and other programs. There may be ministries for financial consulting, male members, female members, seniors, global worship, and a host of other areas. These ministries are smaller targeted programs. Because mega-churches have so many members, they develop smaller programs that can be tailored to different segments of the congregation. This is done to develop a structure in which as many members as possible feel they are active members of the church and not lost in a large congregation.

In *Better Together: Restoring the American Community*, Putnam and Feldstein explore this use of small groups to ensure members feel they are a part of the church:

In any large organization, people's sense of loyalty, connection, and identification comes from being part of a smaller team or group who spend enough time together to know and be known to one another. Joining a small group is the first, essential step in being part of a mega-church rather than just attending it. In his book on the phenomenon of very large churches, Lyle Schaller, author of *The Very Large Church: New Rules for Leaders* (2000), notes, "Most very large congregations affirm the fact that they are a congregation of congregations, of choirs, circles, cells, classes, fellowships, groups, and organizations or a congregation of communities." And in article in the *Atlantic Monthly*, Charles Trueheart cites Jim Mellado of Willow Creek on the importance of lay-led "cells" of up to ten people, the small-group cell being "the basic unit of church life." The same is true at Saddleback. Warren writes, "People are not looking for a friendly *church* as much as they are looking for *friends*." He adds, "The average church member knows 67 people in the congregation, whether the church has 200 or 2,000 attending. A member does not have to know everyone in the church in order to feel it's their church, but he or she does have to know *some* people."[16]

Mega-church leaders lead the rapid growth of their churches by virtue of their charisma, authoritativeness, and ability to personally attract new members. They are articulate, well-versed in secular and religious matters, and convincing in their calls for people to follow them. They command a great deal of respect from their congregations and others outside of their church. They have the same attraction as business and political leaders to persuade, motivate, and convince others. They are people others want to be near, trust, and emulate, and their popularity often reaches celebrity status. They boast of the different, nontraditional, or overwhelming experience their churches can offer in contrast to any others. They are the single dominant figure in their churches and few mega-churches survive after the leader is no longer at the church's helm. The fact that these churches collapse after the exodus of their church leader speaks to the power of the leader.

These leaders are highly paid, and have a dedicated staff of assistant ministers and workers. Mega-churches often have multimillion-dollar budgets, an average of 50 to 60 paid staff members, and thousands of volunteers. For example, in 2009, the 24,000-member Southern Baptist Church of Houston, Texas, had an annual budget of $53 million.[17] When churches grow to the size of mega-churches, they eventually hire a staff of ministers and administrative staff members. The church then hires an executive pastor to serve as chief administrator of the church. Colleen Pepper conducted a survey that drew responses from 555 executive pastors serving in congregations with weekly attendance ranging from 100 to 23,000. Her survey focused on analyzing the following questions: "What does a 'typical' week look like for an executive pastor? How does their role change with their church's size? What factors help them most in having a successful relationship with the senior pastor and with other staff? Where do they struggle most?"[18] The following are some of her primary findings:

- On average, executive pastors work about 50 hours a week, have nine staff directly reporting to them, and spend 40 percent of their time in administration and meetings, including staff supervision. In fact, after financial concerns, staffing and human resources issues top the list in terms of topics executive pastors find themselves thinking about after their heads hit the pillow at night.[19]
- Nearly one-third of responders (28%) indicated having no theological training. Meanwhile, 70 percent indicated they had spent at least five years in a nonchurch field, with "business" ranking much higher than "education," "military" or "other." Among those who do have theological training, 34 percent indicated holding a master's degree, and another 12 percent said they had a degree from a Bible college.[20]
- On the whole, executive pastors report being largely happy and satisfied at work and in their personal lives ... Most report taking a day and a half to

two days off each week, are with their families for dinner four to five nights a week, and say they are "satisfied" or "very satisfied" with their family relationships, including their marriages.[21]

The primary and satellite locations of mega-churches are placed close to areas containing their target market: developing cities with vibrant urban centers. This includes Atlanta, Houston, Dallas/Ft. Worth, Oklahoma City, Nashville, and Orlando. Most mega-churches are located in the suburb of a major city, but some are also in the downtown areas of major cities. The majority are located in the Sunbelt states, with nearly half in the Southeast. This is not surprising given the South has a long and rich history of religion being at the foundation of its culture. Georgia leads the south with the most mega-churches. In 2005, California led the nation with 178 mega-churches. Most of them were concentrated in and around Los Angeles, San Diego, and San Francisco. California was followed by 157 in Texas, and 85 in Florida.[22]

The locations of mega-churches are chosen to allow them to expand their facilities but be near major interstates or other thoroughfares. The church then takes advantage of convenient transportation routes to access a large population of potential new members, particularly those that are middle-class, educated, and mobile. Building large churches near heavily populated areas attracts new members because they are interested and curious. The modern construction and facilities of mega-churches are then specifically geared to appeal to their target audience. Services are held in spacious auditoriums with theater seating, a central large stage, jumbotron screens, and colorful decor, but few (if any) religious symbols. To appear less traditional, they intentionally limit the use of traditional religious symbols (e.g., crosses).

Beyond the main worship area are additional amenities that support the church's many programs and member entertainment. These churches have offices, day-care centers, schools, and courtyards. For example, Second Baptist Church in Houston, Texas, has five campuses for its 24,000 members and operates on an annual budget of $53 million. Its main site is the size of an airport terminal. The church has a fitness center, bookstores, information desks, café, and K-12 school, and it offers free automotive repair for single mothers. The church was built in 1986 at a cost of $34 million.[23]

Mega-churches offer an array of nontraditional church activities to attract members, for example, concerts, book clubs, sports facilities and events, cafés, scout troops, teen and young adult programs, and social groups. In supporting and servicing their local communities, they provide an array of services as part of what Schaller refers to in *The Seven-Day-a-*

Week Church as their "seven-day-a-week" ministries.[24] These services include tutorial and educational programs, health clinics, job networks, psychological counseling, and a diverse array of self-help services. They also support their communities through the funds they generate and their members frequenting local restaurants, gas stations, hotels, and other local businesses. In *Church History in Plain Language*, Shelley described the rise of mega-churches and their full array of services. He wrote that

> with the decline of denominations in American public life and the increasing privatization of religion, large churches gained an increasing share of churchgoing America, or as some crassly called it "the religious market." These large churches grew, at least in part, because they shed the negative image of denominational Christianity and appealed to the popular religious tastes. Like the 76 million members of the post–World War II generation, "mega-churches" like to think of themselves as independent and highly individualized. With attendees in the thousands, Sunday morning services in these churches were usually "full-service" assemblies. But their buildings were filled the rest of the week, too, with Bible classes, support groups, field trips for seniors, weight-loss classes, and children's activities.[25]

The majority of mega-churches are not part of a religious organization such as churches under the Roman Catholic Church, but rather are solitary entities that operate under their own religious ideology and church rules. Most mega-churches are either nondenominational (34%) or downplay their religious affiliation (which is why they purposely do not display religious symbols). This is done to attract members who are adverse to the concept of organized religion and to attract members from various faiths who were formerly dissatisfied members of other churches. Of the mega-churches that do identify as being part of an established religion, the majority are Southern Baptist (16%) or unspecified Baptist (10%).

While the sermon or lecture by the church leader is the primary focus of the religious message, the worship service often includes such nontraditional components as interpretive dancers, mimes, religious rock bands, videos, skits, and step dancers. The structure of each service is carefully choreographed to excite and motivate attendees. Services are also "toned down," with casual dress, lectures rather than hell-and-brimstone sermons, and programs designed for all ethnicities.

Members of mega-churches also share similar characteristics. A third of those who attend are single compared with 10 percent at a typical church, and the average age is 40 compared with 53, respectively. As discussed earlier, mega-churches employ aggressive advertising campaigns to target young members. This is done to foster the future survival of the church. Many organized religions are waning in size due to a reduction of membership and the inability to maintain their youth as they grow older. For example, when the United Methodist Church was formed in 1968 (by the merger of the Methodist Church and the United Evangelical Brethren) it had almost 11 million members in 41,901 congregations in the United States. By 2007, membership was down to approximately 7.8 million in 34,136 congregations.[26] The church enlarged its membership beginning in 2008 by expanding membership overseas. Both the Roman Catholic and Presbyterian Churches are also seeing membership declines in the United States. One reason is because adults in America are switching religions, rather than remaining committed to a single religion as their parents and grandparents did. They are changing their church membership, and also their denominational affiliation, or deciding not to attend services at all.

The Pew Forum on Religion and Public Life interviewed more than 35,000 Americans age 18 and older. Their *U.S. Religious Landscape Survey* found that "more than one-quarter of American adults (28%) have left the faith in which they were raised in favor of another religion—or no religion at all. If change in affiliation from one type of Protestantism to another is included, roughly 44 percent of adults have either switched religious affiliation, moved from being unaffiliated with any religion to being affiliated with a particular faith, or dropped any connection to a specific religious tradition altogether."[27]

Contrary to typical churches, the members of mega-churches are of different races, ethnicities, education levels, income levels, and backgrounds. Their memberships represent the diversity of their local communities, but their members are predominantly educated and in the middle class. Twenty-six percent of families who attend mega-churches earn more than $100,000 a year, compared with 15 percent at typical churches. They therefore seek membership in organizations, including churches, that are in congruence with their desired lifestyle, which are progressive, modern, and dynamic. They attended large universities or work for large companies, and are therefore accustomed to being part of large organizations under the leadership of a charismatic figurehead. From childhood, Americans in general shop in large malls, frequent mega–entertainment centers, and travel on interstates and in huge airports. All of this teaches them how to navigate large congested areas and feel socially comfortable. People even develop a comfort level of being around a large group of people rather than small groups. To remain inconspicuous, then, some join these churches because of their size. Others join churches that are trendy: their church of choice is popular and other members are coworkers or people they aspire to be around or be like. They find prestige in stating they are a member of a certain church and they are affiliated with the church leader.

With all of the aforementioned positive aspects of mega-churches in catering to their members, mega-churches and their leaders also have negative aspects that have drawn criticisms. Among these are sacrificing religion to attract large congregations, church leaders using millions of dollars raised by the church for personal purposes, and their attempts to influence politics and governmental decision making. However, as mega-churches have grown in number and size, their greatest challenge and criticisms have resulted from the actions of their church leaders. Growing incidents of sexual misconduct by heads of mega-churches have caused national concern due to the impact on victims, the betrayal of perpetrators in their positions of trust over so many people, and the resulting negative impact on perceptions of faith and religion by society in general. Numerous mega-church ministers have been engaged in such acts as having sex with minors, having extramarital affairs, and soliciting prostitutes. Because a mega-church leader is the single face and head of his or her church, the leader's actions stigmatize the entire church membership. Often, these actions lead to the collapse of the church. This is the subject of the remainder of the book.

Chapter 2

Mega-Church Leaders: Sex over Faith and Accountability?

PROFILE OF MEGA-CHURCH LEADERS

Mega-churches can be described as the Wal-Marts of churches because of their size and impact on smaller churches. Each mega-church offers a variety of services and programs to its members under a single theological framework and is detrimental to the survival of small churches. Mega-churches have thousands of members, with some having congregations that span the globe due to satellite locations and the use of television, radio, and the Internet. They offer a variety of spiritual programs and have sporting events; some are so large that their campuses include retail stores, restaurants, and schools. This is all done to provide for individuals' and families' religious and social needs, all through the church.

Although they are nonprofit entities, they operate multi-million dollar budgets. Because of their finances and program offerings, they engage in marketed branding that is similar to corporations. This branding is tailored to their uniqueness in comparison to competitors, that is, other churches and denominations. Their brand is tied to the image, message, and theology of the mega-church leader. In essence, this brand is based on how this minister can provide spiritual happiness and salvation unlike any other. Based on the same concept of supply and demand, the minister tailors himself or herself and the church to meet the spiritual and social needs of current and future members. This tailoring is based on extensive research of how to get people into the church and retain them through product placement, attractive slogans, and entertaining experiences.

This speaks to the reality of the capitalistic nature of the United States and most of the Western world: religion, like most other commodities, has now become a competitive market. As discussed by Einstein in *Brands of Faith: Marketing Religion in a Commercial Age*, "Faith brands, like their secular counterparts, exist to aid consumers in making and maintaining a personal connection to a commodity product. Introducing, sustaining, and perpetuating the brand across product lines allow these faith brands to be 'top of mind' in an overcrowded commercial environment. It seems inevitable that branding would occur since these institutions are competing not only among themselves, but also with the popular culture."[1]

Mega-churches brand themselves in order to make potential members want to be a part of their congregation. They not only market based on religion, but also upon the concept of social popularity that comes with being a member of their church. Think of those who speak with pride when they say, "I attended Harvard" or "I work for IBM." Mega-churches seek to instill that same pride when a member says, "I attend Mega-church X, and Minister Y is my pastor!"

Just as Wal-Mart causes smaller stores to close when it moves into a community, mega-churches have the same effect on smaller churches. Smaller churches are already struggling, and an estimated 50 close each week.[2] Mega-churches are making the future plight of those that are struggling to survive even bleaker. Smaller churches just cannot compete with the religious and social offerings of mega-churches (i.e., the one-stop shopping) and have nowhere near the financial resources that are raised by mega-churches from member tithes and outside donations. Smaller churches also cannot compete with the appeal and glamour of mega-churches. When these smaller churches are forced to close, their members join mega-churches. As will be discussed in later sections, this "sheep stealing" is one of the primary criticisms of mega-churches.

Mega-churches also share a key factor in common: they are led by a single leader who serves as the minister, "bishop," or pastor. Ministers of mega-churches are the primary focus of their marketing and member attraction. Their image is carefully crafted to portray the virtues of religious fortitude and virtue, but also personal appeal, confidence, trust, and secular success. These leaders either founded a small church that grew into a mega-church or were selected as leader during the church's early beginnings and led in expanding the church's congregation from a few hundred to thousands of members.

The primary personal characteristic mega-church leaders share is an innate capability to attract followers through their message and their personal attraction or charisma. Their ability to excite and influence so many propels these leaders to celebrity status both within and outside of their churches and localities. Some have served as spiritual advisors to business leaders, governors, senators, and even presidents of the United States. Reverend Joel Hunter of Northland Church in Florida served as a spiritual advisor to President Barack Obama. Mrs. Obama spoke at his church in February 2012 to promote her national program against adult and childhood obesity. Ted Haggard, former minister of New Life Church in Colorado Springs, Colorado, was an evangelical advisor to President George W. Bush. Some mega-church leaders are now even writing best-selling books as well as writing scripts and producing movies. For example, Bishop T. D. Jakes produced the movie *Jumping the Broom*, which was released in 2011. The movie's estimated budget was $6.6 million, but it grossed over $37 million in box office sales.[3] In 2011, Reverend Joel Osteen reported he had signed an agreement to work with producer Mark Burnett to develop a reality show that would feature him taking mission trips with members of his Houston-based Lakewood Church. The program would also feature Osteen's wife, Victoria. Burnett is best known for producing the popular television show *Survivor*. Both Jakes and Osteen have written books that have topped the *New York Times* best-selling list.

Who specifically are mega-church leaders? Approximately 9 percent of the ministers or pastors of mega-churches are men.[4] The average leader is over 50 years of age and has been in his position for 12 years. Half have assumed their positions since 1997. The majority are white (88%), and almost all have a college degree, with 73 percent holding a seminary degree or higher.[5] Mega-church leaders make millions of dollars a year from their churches, gifts from individuals and organizations outside the church, speaking engagements, and sales from their books, DVDs, and CDs. They also host and speak at conferences and on television, and are paid for guest appearances at other churches. In the largest of these churches, ministers make so much money outside of the church (e.g., from books and speaking) that they decline to take a salary from their church.

As part of their business-driven structures, mega-churches do not rely just on donations from members. They are continuously developing innovative and unique strategies to increase their influence and bases of revenues. Take one example outlined in a 2005 *Businessweek* article:

Once established, some ambitious churches are making a big business out of spreading their expertise. Willow Creek Community Church in South Barrington, Ill., formed a consulting arm called Willow Creek Assn. It earned $17 million last year, partly by selling marketing and management advice to 10,500 member churches from 90 denominations. Jim Mellado, the hard-charging Harvard MBA who runs it, last year brought an astonishing 110,000 church and lay leaders to conferences on topics such as effective leadership. "Our entrepreneurial impulse comes from the Biblical mandate to get the message out," says Willow Creek founder Bill Hybels, who hired Stanford MBA Greg Hawkins, a former McKinsey & Co. consultant, to handle the church's day-to-day management. Willow Creek's methods have even been lauded in a Harvard Business School case study.[6]

Mega-church leaders appear to begin their ministries extremely dedicated to their faith and expanding their ministries. However, they are all affected somehow as their churches expand. Some are overwhelmed by the number of members, amount of money they must be financially responsible for, media attention, or amount of personal attention. Most handle these and other pressures by turning to their faith, putting their energies into further expanding their church, relying on family and friends for support, or other positive means. However, some engage in questionable or illegal behavior, including embezzling, misappropriating church funds, using their positions for personal gain, influencing politics, or engaging in sexual misconduct. Growing incidents of the latter have caused concern and even outrage among churchgoers, communities, legal officials, the media, and government officials.

The reasons for these leaders committing acts of sexual misconduct are varied but inherent in their positions as leaders of mega-churches; that is, their position provides them the opportunity to act upon behaviors that were psychologically preexistent or that formulated as a result of the opportunities their position provided. Because of these and other reasons mentioned later, they forgo their responsibilities of devoutness in their role as church leader for personal gratification through sexual misconduct. In many cases, as will also be discussed later, ministers' acts of sex abuse or misconduct are not about the sex itself but rather to feed their personal need for power. This chapter will discuss the reasons and types of sexual misconduct that occur, with examples of actual incidents.

It is important to note in this chapter and throughout the book that sexual misconduct will be discussed from the point of view of the perpetrator being male. Of course, sexual abuse and other acts of sexual misconduct are perpetrated by both men and women. However, this book addresses men because they commit the most acts. As explained by Grenz and Bell in *Betrayal of Trust: Confronting and Preventing Clergy Sexual Misconduct,* "Although in our day sexual misconduct is overwhelmingly an abuse of male power, it is neither exclusively nor intrinsically so, as [psychologist Peter] Rutter seems to imply. The editors of *Psychology Today* are closer to the truth: 'In fact sexual exploitation takes place in all gender combinations, in heterosexual and homosexual varieties.' Sexual misconduct is not inherently connected to the abuse of male power. Rather, it has become a problem of male power, because power remains largely lodged with males in the professionals, in our society and certainly in most churches."[7] The reader should be mindful that although this book discusses sexual misconduct where the perpetrator is male, all of the discussions can also apply to female perpetrators. The reader should also keep in mind that sexual misconduct in the context of this book is synonymous with sexual abuse given the perpetrator: a minister. Whether in unwanted or consensual sex acts with another person, a minister is always in a position of power, and by engaging in sex acts with church members is also abusing or betraying his position as church leader.

POWER OVER FAITH

The power of mega-church leaders is undeniable. Most are the leaders of the church they started with only a very small amount of money, a handful of members, and a vision. During interviews, they recount how they grew their churches from a few members in their living rooms or a small rented space to a congregation of thousands. They also confess they never dreamed they would reach the level of success they have achieved. With their success comes power through influence, money, and respect. With this power, they are able to shape the theological perceptions of their members and thousands outside of their churches based upon their teachings and religious programs. Most are able to use this power in positive ways to serve their communities, countries, and even the world. However, some use this power for personal gain and satisfaction that is contrary to their espoused theology. As stated by historian, politician, and writer John Emerich Edward Dalberg-Acton, 1st Baron Acton of Aldenham, "Power tends to corrupt, and absolute power corrupts absolutely." Sexual misconduct is one of the most negative abuses of their power.

Sexual misconduct by mega-church ministers and religious leaders in general takes many forms. These include extramarital affairs, seeking the services of prostitutes, rape or molestation of an adult, child sex abuse, sexual harassment, and promiscuity. As will be discussed in examples of actual cases throughout the book, these forms of sexual misconduct are perpetrated against those of the opposite or same sex. For religious figures, it also to a lesser extent includes visiting pornographic Internet sites or bookstores, purchasing pornographic literature from other locations, and such violations as self-gratifying oneself while secretly spying on someone.

There are different types of ministerial sex offenders along a continuum of those new to the ministry and those with years of experience. This continuum also ranges from those who do not intentionally do wrong to those that are fully aware of the damage they are doing to themselves and the other party. In their book *Restoring the Soul of a Church: Healing Congregations Wounded by Clergy Sexual Misconduct,* Laaser and Hopkins define six archetypal descriptions of ministerial sexual offenders:[8]

- *The Naïve Prince:* Early in his ministry, this man feels the power of his newly ordained status and feels invulnerable. He meets one or a few congregational members with whom he develops close and unique relationships in which he attempts to fill multiple personal and professional roles. Commonly, congregants are women with challenging or difficult personal problems who possess a specific psycho-dynamic profile the clergyman finds challenging, provocative, intoxicating, and intriguing. Interaction intensifies and exposes vulnerabilities in each of them, to which each responds. Subsequently, a blurring of appropriate professional boundaries leads to sexual misconduct. The clergyman comes to recognize he is involved with a congregant in a relationship far more complex and problematic than he had intended or anticipated, and within a short period of time, the relationship's sexual nature is discovered or reported by one of the involved parties.
- *The Wounded Warrior:* Following completion of training and ordination, a clergyman in this category usually commits much effort and energy to serving his congregation and church. He ventures into the world and becomes engrossed in a demanding ministry. Social life and personal needs are relegated to secondary status, as they were during seminary matriculation. He may be married with children, but his personal validation and self-worth come from this church-endowed mantle, coupled with a personal drive to serve others as a means to maintain self-worth and repress personal shame. He comes to experience existential conflict, and repressed wounds from his past emerge and manifest in new expressions of vulnerability. Professional and social demands combine with internal struggles and lead him to become sexually or romantically involved with one or more congregants or professional staff.
- *The Self-serving Martyr:* Clergymen in this category have progressed to middle or late career stages and in the process have sacrificed personal growth and family involvement for ministry and service in the church and community. Work becomes the primary life activity and the only way to meet personal needs for affirmation and validation. Over time, innate woundedness becomes expressed in sexual and/or romantic relationships within the congregation. The martyr views himself as a suffering servant of

others who do not appreciate how consumed he has become in his professional duties and his service to the church and community. His lament can often be heard in words such as, "I've done so much for so many for so long that I deserve something for me." He becomes angry, resentful, and isolated, often taking on the self-anointed role of prophet-victim. He makes rationalized and justified exceptions to ethical standards and professional boundaries with "special" people, characterized by emotional enmeshment and a blurring of the roles he plays in their lives. Ritualistic grooming progresses to sexual misconduct and offense, often with a series of congregants over significant periods of time.

- *The False Lover:* In reaching adulthood and then attaining professional success, a man may advance his desire to live a life of intensity and continuous high drama. While maintaining professional status and social respectability, the clergyman indulges in the loves and appetites of his body and mind, enjoying life on the edge and the thrill of seducing another in the fulfillment of passion and conquest. Although he may be dramatic, a perfectionist, and enthusiastic in his ministry, he may often be seen to represent a *peur aeternus*, one who has remained too long in adolescent psychology. He becomes captivated by a series of women, each of whom appears for a while to meet his image of perfection. But each is soon found to be ordinary and mundane. His preoccupation with one dissipates, and he moves on to project his ideals and desires on another, hoping she might satisfy his every need.

- *The Dark King:* This clergyman is adept in the exploitation of power for personal aggrandizement and gain. Socially skilled and verbally facile, he appears charming and charismatic. Using rational and refined arguments, he convinces those he serves that he possesses special abilities. He is dynastic and driven by grandiosity as well as a pathological need to control and dominate. Once confronted and exposed, he is someone you will never forget. He initially experiences professional success and renown. With experience and greater resources at his disposal, he becomes more deliberate, cunning, and manipulative. Sexual exploitation represents an expression of power, superiority, and dominance. Victims are carefully chosen to meet his sexual agenda and interests.

- *The Wild Card:* These clergymen have an erratic, unpredictable course their in personal and professional lives. At some point in their career, usually prior to allegations of sexual impropriety, they experience significant difficulty in functioning effectively, seek professional help, and are diagnosed with a major mental health disorder on Axis 1 in the *DSM-IV* (*Diagnostic and Statistical Manual of Mental Disorders*). Subsequent treatment often brings improvement, and the clergyman may perform well for period of time before there is a return to mental illness. Following the relapse, it is often discovered that the clergyman has engaged in sexual impropriety. Sexual acting out occurs when management of the primary disorder is not optimal. This acting out is often associated with poor social judgment and loose professional boundaries. The dynamics of exploitation are often less ritualized, premeditated, or easily defined.

In *Before the Fall: Preventing Pastoral Sexual Abuse*, Friberg and Laaser also discuss the characteristics of ministers that commit sexual abuse. They state these sex offenders can be placed on a continuum from "wanderers" to "sexual predators."[9] The first are naïve and cross sexual boundaries but are ignorant of the damage they have done. They view their actions as random sexual encounters that are not meant to hurt anyone. At the other end of the continuum are sexual predators. They are aware of the damage they do, are sociopathic in their actions, and lack awareness of the harm they cause. Friberg and Laaser also list the following traits of all sexual abusers in the ministry that appear somewhere along this continuum: controlling, dominating, limited self-awareness, limited or no awareness of boundary issues, no sense of damage caused by their own behavior, poor judgment, limited impulse control, limited understanding of consequences of their actions, often charismatic, sensitive, talented, inspirational and effective in ministry, limited or no awareness of their own power, lack of recognition of their own sexual feelings, and confusion of sex and affection. They state that ministers with these characteristics may cause problems for their congregations even before any sexual misconduct occurs. For example, they may make erratic decisions based solely on personal preference, be unconcerned about the repercussions of damaging statements, or exert such extreme control over the church that they develop paranoid tendencies whenever their directions are questioned.

Many of the traits mentioned by Friberg and Laaser have been used to describe mega-church ministers. They are charismatic, which allows them to attract so many people to follow them. They are very effective in their ministries, as evidenced by their large congregations and ability to influence local and national issues and leaders. They are often not aware of their own power. As stated earlier, many state they never set out to start a church of thousands of members and were caught off guard by their own ability to attract so many to their church. They are obviously controlling and sometimes dominating because they have to lead so many and maintain oversight over a staff of sometimes hundreds as well as multi-million dollar budgets.

In the case of sexual misconduct, the negative traits outlined earlier in this chapter are also evident. There is clearly a lack of understanding of the importance of maintaining boundaries between themselves and others, both in terms of physical boundaries and emotional boundaries connected the role of being a minister. At the same time, they are often not aware of the damage their actions cause their victims. When misconduct issues become public, they speak to their innocence. Often this is thought to be simply their denial of their actions in order to protect themselves from persecution and prosecution. But this denial may also stem from believing they really have not done anything wrong. Some also lack impulse control. They continually abuse minors over the course of decades, repeatedly seek the services of prostitutes, or engage in multiple extramarital affairs for years.

Some divulged incidents of sexual misconduct involve ministers who do not recognize their own sexual feelings because of sexual ambiguity and/or denial. This may be especially true of those who engage in homosexual affairs while at the same time publicly denouncing homosexuality. Finally, those who engage in sexual misconduct often cause other negative issues for the church as well. They embezzle money, instigate dissention among members and staff, persuade their members to support positions that cast the church in a negative political and social light, and constantly strive to maintain power over every aspect of the church through control, manipulation, and threats.

Power is the primary reason mega-church leaders commit acts of sexual misconduct. They do so for the same reason leaders of government, business, and entertainment do. Their position of power gives them the means, opportunity, and inclination. Even when a minister engages in consensual sex, many characterize this as abuse of power for sexual gain that is just as morally and legally wrong as rape or child molestation because it results in sex gained through unbalanced persuasion or outright coercion. As discussed by Laaser in *Healing the Wounds of Sexual Addiction,*

In addition to rape, and child molestation, abuse of authority is another exploitive and criminal sexual activity. This includes sexual activity between two adults not biologically related, when one of them is in the position of greater power or authority, such as a doctor, lawyer, teacher, employer, or older adult. This is sometimes referred to as "authority rape." Although the person [victim] may have consented to or even initiated the sexual activity, the consent or the initiation is not freely given because the situation is inequitable when one person has greater influence or emotional power over the other. In these situations the person not in power is the victim.[10]

As will be discussed in greater detail later, congregants who engage in what they may believe is consensual sex with a mega-church leader are in essence victims. This is because they do not have control or influence over what the primary factors of the relationship are: the means, the opportunity, and the mutual inclination of both parties. The minister controls when and where they will meet, the facets of the sexual relationship, and for how long the relationship will last. This control is inherent in the minister's position of power.

Renowned German sociologist Max Weber defined power as "the probability that one actor within a social relationship will be in a position to carry out his own will despite resistance, regardless of the basis on which this probability rests."[11] Normal actors, or normal people in the course of their everyday lives, weigh the alternatives of the consequences of their actions and the probability of each consequence occurring. Those in power do not. Any basic course in management or leadership outlines the five sources, or bases, of power. The following are the five sources and how they are present in cases of mega-church leaders' sexual misconduct:[12]

- *Legitimate power:* Power granted through the organizational hierarchy that allows a person to give subordinates orders that they will follow. The mega-church leader has this power by virtue of being spiritual leader of his church; his subordinates include members of the church staff who can be fired for noncompliance and church members who can be asked to leave the church.

- *Reward power:* Power to give or withhold rewards such as salaries, bonuses, promotions, praise, recognition, and preferred job assignments. Mega-church leaders control church resources, decide which assignments to give church staff and members, can give wanted praise and recognition in public or in private, and have the reward power of instilling spiritual happiness through support and recognition.

- *Coercive power:* Power to force compliance through psychological, emotional, or physical threat. Mega-church ministers have extreme psychological power through their words and the verbal ability to manipulate others into compliance. They can instill emotional shame by pointing to a person's spiritual failings or failings to provide adequate support to the church or to the minister; they can also use the threat of physical force that they or someone else will inflict if a person does not comply with their wishes (such as physically threatening a child's parents if the child does not engage in sex).

- *Referent power:* Power through identification, imitation, or charisma. The primary ability of mega-church leaders to become so successful is through the charisma that is inherent in their personality and attitude. They are able to motivate others and inspire enthusiasm; their followers want to imitate how they think, what they wear, and how they live. Followers also want to espouse their minister's theological philosophies in how they approach religion, live their lives, interact with others, and view themselves in the context of their social and cultural surroundings.

- *Expert power:* Power through information and expertise. A mega-church leader serves as the primary expert on the Bible, the church's theology, and how religion should guide a person's life.

Based upon these sources of power, a leader can properly use or manipulate this power in several ways:

- *Legitimate requests:* Asking members of the church or staff members to perform duties or actions that are appropriately within the realm of religiously, socially, culturally, and legally appropriate behavior (e.g., asking church members to attend service each Sunday or take part in programs that support the community).
- *Instrumental compliance:* Rewarding church members or staff when they comply with a request. This may include positive compliance in which they are rewarded through praise or money for completing acceptable tasks, or it can include compliance with negative requests such as sex or personal favors that violate moral or legal standards.
- *Coercion:* Gaining compliance through the use of punishment in the form of withholding rewards or inflicting negative consequences. As will be discussed later, coercion is the primary method used in acts of sexual misconduct.
- *Rational persuasion:* Persuading a church or staff member that their compliance is in their best interests. This method is similar to reward power except the leader does not control the reward (such as another person's feeling of sexual gratification).
- *Personal identification:* A church leader exploits a person's personal identification with the leader for the leader's own benefit, for example, taking advantage of a minor's feeling that the leader serves as a role model.
- *Inspirational appeal:* A minister exploits a person's feeling of loyalty to the leader. In this case, the minister persuades a person to do something by insisting his behavior is consistent with the person's obligation to their higher beliefs or values.
- *Information distortion:* A leader withholds or distorts certain information to obtain a desired behavior.

Any form of these sources or types of power leads to dominance by a church minister over others through power manipulation. Weber further defines dominance as a more carefully defined concept and "as the probability that certain specific commands (or all commands) will be obeyed by a given group of persons. It thus does not include every mode of exercising power or influence over other persons. Domination (authority) in this sense may be based on the most diverse motives of compliance: all the way from simple habituation to the most purely rational calculation of advantage. Hence every genuine form of domination implies a minimum of voluntary compliance, that is, an interest (based on ulterior motives or genuine acceptance) in obedience."[13]

Dominance exists between supervisors and employees, parents and children, teachers and students, and ministers and church members/staff. There are various sources of power and dominance that ministers posses, giving them the ability to influence others to do what they will. These include power through delegated authority as church leader, social class due to wealth, celebrity status, personal charisma, power of persuasion, ability and skills, and moral persuasion through religion.

Managers and leaders in private businesses derive a great deal of their power through the formal hierarchy of an organization through position descriptions, duties and roles assigned to personnel through their positions, and organizationally established reward systems. Alternatively, ministers derive their power through church members who voluntarily choose to first follow the minister and second to allow him to have persuasive reign over their thinking and actions. While a person may not be able to choose to easily quit a job and certainly not choose who his or her direct supervisor is in a company, a person can easily choose to leave a church or not allow a minister to have control over him or her. An individual's decisions in the latter case are dependent on the minister's level of persuasion and ability to psychologically manipulate thoughts and actions.

Mega-church ministers who do engage in sexual misconduct are not alone in possessing different perceptions of people and their surroundings due to their positions of power. People in power generally see the world differently in terms of their control over other people and situations, especially in romantic sexual situations. They are confident, assertive, and feel they are not bound by some social norms. They are therefore more prone to take risks, such as extramarital affairs, and feel a level of confidence they will not get caught. This confidence also results from a feeling that the other person either cannot or will not resist their advance because of their position and power. According to a study published in *Psychological Science* in 2011,

people in power generally are more confident, self-assured, assertive, and impulsive than people low in power. Recently, researchers found that power's effect on confidence also translates to romantic behavior: Power makes people focus their attention on physically attractive others, it increases romantic approach behavior, and it makes people optimistic in their perception of sexual interest on the part of potential mates. As a result, participants who hold a high-power role in a mixed-sex (male-female) interaction with strangers are more confident and self-assured than participants who are given a low-power role. This increased confidence may even manifest itself in actual increased attractiveness; the outward signs of confidence—direct eye contact, moving close toward other people, a self-assured posture—are associated with increased attractiveness.[14]

From an academic point of view, social exchange theory further explains why some ministers commit acts of sexual misconduct. This theory holds that in human relationships, negotiated exchanges between parties are based upon a subjective cost-benefit analysis and comparing of alternatives. A person will calculate the overall value, outcome, or worth of a relationship with another person based upon comparing the rewards (or benefits) to the costs. Interaction will take place if the rewards outweigh the costs. The rewards include financial gain, increased social status, and personal satisfaction. In the case of mega-church ministers committing sexual misconduct, the rewards are two-fold: sexual gratification and power gratification. The costs include the repercussions of getting caught and the level of effort required to obtain sex from the other person. The drive to obtain the perceived benefits here outweigh the costs in that the minister feels there are low costs related to getting what he wants, a low probability of being caught because of his high level of control over the person and the situation, and a high probability of receiving gratification. The problem in this situation is that the other person is seldom given the opportunity to weigh the costs and benefits. While some would also say the minister may not be using reason and rational thinking in weighing the costs of benefits, to him his choice is both reasonable and rational. As discussed earlier, a minister's position of power causes him see the world differently in terms of control over other people and situations. This distorts his reasoning and rational thinking in comparison to that of a "normal" or "regular" person.

To explain misconduct when there are so many risks, one has to also consider decision making within the context of power and coercion. Power and the resulting ability to coerce others into behavior greatly reduce the costs associated with achieving the benefits. It allows for the controlling of situations, while reducing such risks as public disclosure, subordinate noncompliance, and proximity to rival forces. They can persuade others to comply with their positions regardless of whether they feel committed to it, and they can force followers to accept their power as reasonable and legitimate.

Power is the primary factor leading to sexual harassment in professional and personal settings. It is the same in church settings in that a person in a position of authority uses that position to coerce those in subordinate positions (employees or church members) into sexual situations. In the workplace, power is exerted by controlling subordinates' pay, promotions, and other benefits. In the church, the minister wills this same power for members of the church's staff. For members of the congregation, ministers will power through spiritual or religious manipulation in addition to their position of power as church leader. Their power also rests in the ability to persuade others to conform to their teachings and even manipulate normal behaviors. This is true of all ministers in that their profession is based upon persuading others to change their thinking and behaviors to conform to a particular ideology. The basics of most religions include persuading a person to control their personal choices and abide by such principles as not stealing, not committing adultery, not being jealous, and not killing. Unfortunately, some ministers manipulate their ability to persuade by convincing others to commit acts of sex.

An example of this use of coercion leading to sexual harassment was seen in the alleged activities of Joseph Walker III, pastor of Mt. Zion Baptist Church in Nashville, Tennessee. In 2012, he was first charged with having an affair with the spouse of a church member that lasted for years. The husband of the church member brought the charges and was seeking $5 million in retribution. The couple had sought marriage counseling from Walker soon after they were married, but instead, the husband alleged, Walker began the affair. In a separate case, four female members also alleged sexual misconduct and began a lawsuit seeking $5 million in damages. The husband of one these women also reported that he and his wife sought marriage counseling from the minister beginning in 2000. The counseling also led to Walker beginning an affair with the wife. The lawsuit outlined how Walker used his position of influence to persuade the woman into the affair. He also affirmed his authority during church services by showing photographs of himself with government officials and celebrities, as well as driving his Bentley. The church publicly denied all allegations and affirmed its belief in the minister's innocence.[15]

Just as there are many allegations of power abuse by mega-church leaders, it must be stated that some allegations are opportunistic and false. They are attempts to use a minister's position of power against him. In some cases, false allegations result because a leader has committed a wrongful act in the past. Future allegations are made to take advantage of the situation. For example, in December 2010, televangelist Marcus Lamb, the founder of the Daystar Television Network, admitted on television that he had been involved in an extramarital affair. The Daystar Network not only airs programs by Lamb, but also other high profile mega-church leaders including Joel Osteen, T. D. Jakes, Kenneth

Copeland, and Joyce Meyer. Lamb's extramarital affair had allegedly already ended before he came out publicly, but Daystar funds had been used when he met the woman in various locations. Lamb had kept the matter private on the advice of marriage counselors that going public would not allow Lamb and his wife to heal from the affair, and the couple reconciled. He made the incident public because three former female Daystar employees filed a series of lawsuits against Lamb and his wife with allegations ranging from financial mismanagement (in relation to the affair), to sexual harassment, to wrongful termination. The women asked for $7.5 million in exchange for not making their accusations public.[16] Civil and countersuits ensued between Lamb and the three women until they finally dropped their cases in 2011.

As mentioned earlier, power gives mega-church leaders a greater opportunity to stray and the overconfidence to think they will get away with it. With influence and power over so many people, there is a greater temptation to cheat on spouses or commit worse acts such as child molestation. This power not only instills blind trust in members and others outside of the congregation to believe the church leader will not commit acts of misconduct, but also leads to others being persuaded to engage in acts they normally would not. For example, former pastor Earl Paulk of the Chapel Hill Harvester Church outside of Atlanta, Georgia, manipulated a church employee into having an affair with him from 1989 until 2003 by telling her that having sex with him was her only path to salvation. Eddie Long of the New Birth Missionary Church in Georgia was accused of coercing at least one of his young male victims by presiding over a spiritual "covenant" ceremony that was essentially a marriage ceremony with candles, the exchange of jewelry, and the use of biblical quotes to justify his requests. These are prime examples of church leaders using rational persuasion (in the former case) and inspirational appeal (in the latter case) to obtain compliance.

A mega-church leader's power and influence is not simply a manner of falsely manifested self-confidence; it is real. A single person has the lead in the growth of a church from a few hundred members to thousands by the single virtue of his personal charisma and influence. This creates a tremendous inflation of self-confidence, self-worth, and self-importance. In a healthy psyche, these feelings can be somewhat controlled and channeled to continue doing good things. In an unhealthy psyche, these feelings may lead the individual to see what other actions he can take, for example, manipulation and criminal behavior. These feelings give the minister the confidence to take risks and feel he will be able to overcome any obstacles. Sexual misconduct is but one of many actions he may engage in.

Former televangelist and Assemblies of God minister Jim Bakker is an example of a minister who knowingly abused his power is several ways. Bakker and his former wife, Tammy Faye, were the hosts of the PTL (Praise the Lord) Club. At the height of their success, their television ministry was shown on hundreds of stations to 12 million viewers. In the 1980s, they constructed Heritage USA, a theme park in Fort Mill, South Carolina, and established the PTL Television Network. From 1984 through 1987, Bakker sold $1,000 lifetime memberships to supporters that entitled them to a three-night stay each year at a new luxury hotel at the theme park. Although tens of thousands of memberships were sold, the completed hotel had only 500 rooms. Millions of dollars were personally kept by Bakker, and the remainder of the money was used for operating expenses. He personally managed the church and park's accounting. It was later revealed that he made a $279,000 payoff to a staff secretary of the church, Jessica Hahn, in exchange for her silence about a sexual incident. Hahn claimed that Bakker and another minister raped her. Bakker acknowledged meeting her in a hotel room in Clearwater Beach, Florida, but denied he raped her. However, the scandal forced him to resign from his church in 1987. Bakker was then charged in a 28-page indictment on eight counts of mail fraud, 15 counts of wire fraud, and one count of conspiracy in 1988 after a 16-month federal grand jury probe. After a five-week trial in 1989, a jury found him guilty of all 24 counts; he was sentenced to 45 years in prison and fined $500,000. His sentence was reduced to eight years in 1992. In August 1993, he was transferred to a minimum security federal prison in Jesup, Georgia, and was subsequently granted parole in July 1994, after serving almost five years of his sentence. After the Hahn scandal in 1987, Bakker was replaced in the church by Jerry Falwell. Rather than supporting Bakker, Falwell called him a liar, an embezzler, a sexual deviant, and "the greatest scab and cancer on the face of Christianity in 2,000 years of church history."[17]

The power and influence of mega-church leaders also manifests itself in the self-confidence that leader will be able to convince or control the person he is cheating with from telling. The behavior can become addictive. If a minister gets away with a first incident, this gives him the confidence to do it again. There are several reasons for this. First, the leader believes no one will believe victims if they tell. If they do tell others, ministers have the money and influence to discredit them or simply pay them off. Second, they are given more options by virtue of people wanting to have sex with them. Women and men are attracted to people in power and will give them a level of attention that they would not if the leader were an average person. They will also look for what benefits they can gain financially and socially by having sex with the leader. Third, this position of power is a catalyst to bring out sexually addictive behavior that was already in existence within the psyche of the individual but suppressed by an earlier motivation to do what was right and serve the needs of the church. Types of sexual addictions will be presented later. Last, the leader has the means to easily fulfill these addictive needs outside of the church. Many ministers exposed for sexual misconduct frequented prostitutes, which allowed them to maintain their anonymity. Because they travel so frequently, they have ample opportunity to do so without worrying about scrutiny by the church and local community.

Ted Haggard is an example. Haggard was founder and pastor of the 14,000-member New Life Church in Colorado Springs, Colorado, and president of the National Association of Evangelicals (NAE) from 2003 until 2006. At the time he was president, the NAE represented 30 million evangelical Christians. Haggard was such a powerful religious figure that he regularly met with President George W. Bush and his advisors. Haggard devoutly condemned homosexuality. In 2006, a male prostitute claimed that Haggard had been in a relationship with him for three years and that he had given Haggard methamphetamine during their sexual encounters. The prostitute knew Haggard only by an alias until he saw him on television and realized who he was. Rather than attempting to blackmail him, the male prostitute decided to go public. Haggard resigned from the NAE and was fired from the church. In January 2009, he admitted to having another homosexual relationship with a church member. The member was in his early twenties at the time and reported that the relationship was not consensual. The two met when the young man came to New Life after being dismissed from his former church due to struggles with homosexuality. The young man was surprised and flattered that Haggard took such an interest in helping him, since he wanted to one day become a minister himself. Haggard soon began sending him sexually explicit text messages and made attempts to have sex with him. When the young man revealed this to the church in 2008, he was offered approximately $179,000 for counseling and tuition costs. The young man said he was also told remain publicly silent about the incidents.[18]

As stated earlier, power is often not a lone factor in causing sexual misconduct; rather, it is often a contributing factor to an underlying psychological propensity that already exists. In other words, a position of power gives a person the means to act upon innate feelings. Ephebophiliacs are an example. These are adults who are attracted to or have a sexual preference for mid- to late adolescents, generally between the ages of 15 and 19. Within this age group are boys and girls who are not yet of the legal age for consensual sex with an adult but who have reached or gone through puberty (as distinguished from the victims of pedophiles, who are have yet to reach puberty). Leaders of mega-churches with an attraction to these adolescents have a large population of potential victims within the church, the influence over both parents and their children to gain access to them privately through a false trust, the position of power to influence victim behavior, and the financial means to remove victims from their normal environment. In this respect, ministers are like teachers, coaches, and camp counselors. They have the means, opportunity, and elements of trust to take advantage of their victims.

For example, Eddie Long is alleged to have used his position as senior pastor of New Birth Missionary Baptist Church, a mega-church in DeKalb County, Georgia, to have sex with young males. Long grew the church from 300 members in 1987 to 25,000 by 2011. In 2011, four plaintiffs claimed that Long had coerced them into sex when they were in their teens. Long allegedly began sexual relations with each of them when they were at least 16 years of age. Sixteen is the minimum age for sexual consent in the state of Georgia. The plaintiffs alleged Long placed them on the church's payroll and bought them expensive gifts, including cars. They also claimed he separately took them on elaborate trips to New York, Kenya, South Africa, Trinidad, Honduras, New Zealand, and the Turks and Caicos Islands. Some of these trips were on Long's private jet. On these trips, he coerced them into sleeping with him and would use biblical scripture to justify having sex with them. The majority of the sexual acts took place on the church's property, including inside Long's guest house. The plaintiffs disclosed photographs, emails, and text messages between themselves and Long, and reported Long called them his "spiritual sons." Long admitted to buying them gifts, taking them on trips, and even hugging some of them. However, he denied having sex with them. As part of his ministry, Long was well known for publicly denouncing homosexuality. The revelation of his actions caused national outrage because he long preached he could "cure" homosexuality with counseling while secretly using church resources and his position to coerce the young males into sex. Long was not prosecuted because of his actions; rather, he silenced the youth with out-of-court settlements.

This is not the only issue Long has faced as pastor of New Birth. As stated earlier, ministers who commit acts of sexual misconduct are also prone to committing other violations against the church. The August 28, 2005 edition of the *Atlanta Journal-Constitution* reported that Long received at least $3.07 million in salary, benefits, and the use of property from his charity, Bishop Eddie Long Ministries, Inc., between 1997 and 2000. This amount was nearly half of what the charity gave to all recipients combined. Long's defense was that this compensation was justified because he had to deal with the White House, foreign prime ministers, and presidents all over the world in addition to managing a multi-million dollar church. Lawyers for the church also contended the funds were compensation for the many years Long served as minister of the church but received no pay.[19]

Long's case and others that are similar raise another issue of how ministers who engage in sexual misconduct choose their victims. Often, the victims are in some way demographically, socially or economically disenfranchised. In Long's case, his alleged victims were minors, poor, and from single parent homes. In other reported cases, the victims were psychologically unstable in some way—they were from broken homes, involved in unstable relationships, prostitutes, or poor. Sexual predators choose their victims based upon some vulnerability they see. They then fantasize about how, where, and when they will take advantage of this vulnerability, rehearsing their plan over and over. Often this rehearsal is conducted as part of sex, either through masturbation or with one's spouse. As part of sex, the urge to make the fantasy come true becomes stronger. Power and control drive this urge to bring the fantasy true. This is sometimes mixed with anger at having to hide their true feelings (e.g., being secretly homosexual), having been sexually abused as a child, or some other deeply held resentment. The aspect of power lies in being able to control the victim by manipulating him or her sexually through the vulnerability.

The opportunity to take advantage of the victim is often not difficult given that most victims of sexual abuse know the perpetrator, who is often a family member, work associate, teacher, friend of the family, or minister. For example, 90 percent of child victims know their offender. Ministers know their members as well as their families, along with personal information about them. Just as in other abuse cases, a minister establishes rapport with his potential victim. This is done through counseling sessions, church functions, trips, meals, or a visit to the minister's home. The perpetrator begins giving his potential victim special attention. This is through long talks, gifts, excessive praise, and other methods that fill the void of the perceived vulnerability. Using his inspirational appeal, reward power, and/or information distortion, the minister preys upon the victim.

As the contact continues, the minister turns to coercion and rational persuasion. The perpetrator begins to test the victim's willingness to have sex through touching, sexual innuendos, and sometimes more forwardly by such methods as offering massages or such acts as showering together. The victim begins to feel uncomfortable but still clings to the special attention that is given. If the victim resists, the perpetrator uses guilt in response. The minister makes such statements as "You're hurting my feelings" or "Don't you think about my feelings?" In some cases, he turns to manipulation by using such methods as distorting scripture to justify his actions or making such claims as the victim's actions will contribute to their spiritual salvation. This is all done to establish control over the victim. Finally, the perpetrator isolates the victim. This occurs by removing the victim from his or her comfort zone, taking him or her somewhere where he or she cannot contact family or friends for help, and taking him or her somewhere the perpetrator has full control by virtue of his being in control of transportation, money, and any financial or physical means to get away or call for help.

At this stage of bringing the sexual act to fruition, the perpetrator uses force, coercion, seduction, or reliance on the inability of the victim to resist. Force involves physically molesting or raping the victim. (In some cases of force, many of the aforementioned actions are not used. It has been reported that some ministers grope their members during baptisms, weddings, and other church ceremonies.) Seduction assumes the victim finds some trait about the perpetrator attractive and is then lured into taking actions based upon a desire that was already in existence. The last issue involves taking advantage of such traits as sex addiction, knowing the person is unable resist the temptation of sex due to a psychological problem. In some cases, ministers rely on the knowledge that the person is being neglected by his or her spouse or parents, and he uses the excuse of showing affection to gain compliance.

Ministers mostly rely on coercion, as it is directly associated with power. As Benyei explains in *Understanding Clergy Misconduct in Religious Systems: Scapegoating, Family Secrets, and the Abuse of Power*, "Coercion is another form of force. Here a different form of power is used and abused—the power of position. Coercion occurs when it is hinted or overtly told to the potential victim that unless he or she cooperates, either (1) something bad will happen, (2) he or she will not get a desired position, and/or will lose his/her present position, or (3) something bad will happen to someone else. Coercion uses fear, financial leverage, and emotional blackmail."[20] The perpetrator also threatens to end his relationship with the victim. This includes no longer giving them attention, gifts, and spiritual support.

The perpetrator acts out the sexual fantasy with little regard for the feelings of his victim. He may act out only a part of the fantasy to test how far the victim will go, at the same time planning his next event in which they will act out more of the fantasy. For the victim, he or she is so stunned and shocked by the event that he or she often detaches mentally from the event. This detachment can be described as having an out-of-body experience in which the victim feels he or she is watching the event from afar. A victim's silence is never a reason to blame him or her for what is happening. The shock and fear of being sexually abused is mentally and physically overwhelming. Silence is a coping mechanism to hide shame and hurt. Silence is also a result of being manipulated into thinking he or she is an active participant in the sexual acts being perpetrated.

After the sexual episode is over, the perpetrator shames or threatens the victim to secrecy. He may threaten to tell others what happened, threaten the victim or his or her family, or threaten to no longer provide gifts or attention. The victim is warned that bad things may happen or that he or she actually was the seducer. The writings of Frawley-O'Dea on sexual abuse in the Roman Catholic Church apply to the same situation in other denominations. As she outlines in *Perversions of Power: Sexual Abuse in the Catholic Church*, secrecy is the acknowledged cornerstone of sexual abuse.

Some perpetrators extract silence by suggesting that victims will be blamed for the abuse, taken from their homes, and placed in an orphanage, or worse ... Perpetrators often threaten the victim's family as well as the minor in order to ensure that the young person will not disclose the abuse. Sexual abusers may also blame the victim, accusing him or her of seducing the predator, effectively ensuring secrecy by filling the victim with the shame and self-loathing more appropriately experienced by the victimizer. Priests abusing girls may have been particularly inclined to blame victims. There is a long tradition in the Roman Catholic Church that views females as seducers capable of making a man lose his mind, as Adam sometimes is depicted as doing when he succumbed to Eve's plea that he eat of the forbidden fruit.[21]

In adults, similar threats take place when the perpetrator threatens the victim as well as his or her husband or wife, children, or parents. The perpetrator also threatens to divulge to the church the victim was actually the seducer, take action to get him or her fired, or ensure he or she is ostracized by the community.

The perpetrator's behavior becomes more aggressive over time, as does his acts during sexual episodes. During future episodes, the perpetrator becomes less and less concerned about the victim's welfare and more concerned about his own sexual gratification. If the victim remains silent and never exposes the perpetrator, the perpetrator may leave the victim alone because his thirst for power has been quenched. He will then seek another victim in persuit of the thrill of exerting power anew. The victim, in turn, may now be susceptible to being abused by others. Victims of sexual abuse are often easily targeted by other perpetrators.

There are many types of sexual predators. Some choose their victims randomly, but most choose people they know. Some chose people who share similar physical characteristics, while others chose victims that have traits similar to someone they know or that they fantasize about. The leaders of mega-churches choose people they know, that can somehow be coerced, and that (the minister believes) will not reveal the incident. Another trait of potential victims appears to be people perpetrators can discredit if incidents are revealed by nature of the person's personal characteristics as well as the circumstances in which incidents occurred. For example, they will explain their being together as part of a church-related trip, the reasons the accuser cannot be trusted (e.g., being raised in a broken home), and why the person may have mistaken their attention or caring as an incorrect indication of sexual attraction. In most cases of sexual misconduct, mega-churches leaders choose secretaries, prostitutes, and minors.

Even consensual sex between a minister and a member of his congregation is not acceptable. The minister holds a position of power over anyone he has a personal relationship with, and within his position of authority, he is charged with protecting his members spiritually. As McClintock explains in *Preventing Sexual Abuse in Congregations: A Resource for Leaders*,

Sexualized contact between a pastor and a parishioner in the context of the ministerial role is never consensual because the clergy person has more power in the relationship. The clergy or staff person could be viewed as sexually harassing the parishioner. The ministerial role includes the daily activities of a pastor in a congregation, such as calling on parishioners, preaching, teaching, counseling, office work, the administration of programs, and conducting worship. In any of these roles a sexualized relationship is not consensual with a child, an adolescent, or an adult, due to the power inherent within the pastoral role. Pastoral responsibilities may also include ministries beyond the local church, such as chaplaincy or pastoral counseling, and specialized duties, such as the supervision of ministerial candidates. Just as there is always a power difference between a minister and a parishioner, a supervisor always has power over a ministerial candidate. Among all of the helping professionals, the clergy role is highly charged with power and authority. The nature of the profession can easily cause a person to project onto the clergy an expectation of saintliness. The pastor is an authority on the word of God and on the "truth." The pastor is the teacher of the Bible and is seen as holding the key to spiritual well-being.[22]

PSYCHOLOGICAL DISORDERS AND SEXUAL ADDICTIONS

Many acts of sexual misconduct result because of psychological disorders that manifest into sexual addictions. In many people, these conditions pre-exist in their psyche due to events that happened during childhood.

They are able to suppress them for years but finally succumb due to a perceived similarity in another person, the ability and opportunity to act upon their condition without perceived repercussions, or a traumatic or stressful event that triggers their behavior. The *Diagnostic Statistical Manual of Mental Disorders* (better known as the *DSM-IV*), published by the American Psychiatric Association, covers all mental health disorders for children and adults. It is used by mental health professionals to diagnose, understand, and treat patients. According to the manual, sexual addictions are classified as such because they are medically considered to cause behaviors that are not consistent with normal behaviors within a given society or culture. They are also urges, behaviors, or thoughts that are outside of a person's control and thus may cause harm to the addicted person and/or others. These addictions are grouped under the general term of *paraphilia*. In medical terms, "Paraphilias all have in common distressing and repetitive sexual fantasies, urges, or behaviors. These fantasies, urges, or behaviors must occur for a significant period of time and must interfere with either satisfactory sexual relations or everyday functioning if the diagnosis is to be made. There is also a sense of distress within these individuals. In other words, they typically recognize the symptoms as negatively impacting their life but feel as if they are unable to control them."[23]

The following are types of sexual addictions:[24]

- *Exhibitionism:* This disorder is characterized by intense sexually arousing fantasies, urges, or behaviors in which the individual exposes his or her genitals to an unsuspecting stranger. To be considered diagnosable, the fantasies, urges, or behaviors must cause significant distress in the individual or be disruptive to his or her everyday functioning. There are different theories related to exhibitionistic behaviors, many stemming from the psychoanalytic camp. They suggest that childhood trauma (e.g., sexual abuse) or significant childhood experiences can manifest in exhibitionistic behavior.
- *Fetishism:* Fetishism is characterized by intense sexually arousing fantasies, urges, or behaviors in which the individual uses a nonliving object (e.g., high heeled shoe, stockings) in a sexual manner. Typically, the individual requires this object to become sexually aroused, that is, he or she is unable to be aroused without it. To be considered diagnosable, the fantasies, urges, or behaviors must cause significant distress in the individual or be disruptive to his or her everyday functioning. Like most disorders in this category, many theories exist to explain how this disorder develops. Most experts agree that underlying issues related to childhood play a major role in the etiology.
- *Frotteurism:* This disorder is characterized by intense sexually arousing fantasies, urges, or behaviors in which the individual touches or rubs

against a nonconsenting person in a sexual manner. This often occurs in somewhat conspicuous situations such as on a crowded bus or subway. To be considered diagnosable, the fantasies, urges, or behaviors must cause significant distress in the individual or be disruptive to his or her everyday functioning. Like most disorders in this category, many theories exist to explain how this disorder develops. Most experts agree that underlying issues related to childhood play a major role in the etiology.

- *Pedophilia:* This disorder is characterized by intense sexually arousing fantasies, urges, or behaviors involving sexual activity with a prepubescent child (typically age 13 or younger). To be considered for this diagnosis, the individual must be at least 16 years old and at least five years older than the child. A large percentage of individuals with this disorder were sexually abused as children, although the vast majority of adults who were abused do *not* develop pedophilia or pedophilic behaviors. Some argue that pedophilia results from feelings of inadequacy with same-age peers, which leads to a transfer of sexual urges to children.

- *Sexual masochism:* Sexually masochistic behaviors are typically evident by early adulthood and often start with masochistic or sadistic play in childhood. The disorder is characterized by intense sexually arousing fantasies, urges, or behaviors in which the individual is humiliated, beaten, bound, or made to suffer in some way. There are different theories related to sexual masochism, many stemming from the psychoanalytic camp. They suggest that childhood trauma (e.g., sexual abuse) or significant childhood experiences can manifest in exhibitionistic behavior.

- *Sexual sadism:* Sexually sadistic behaviors are typically evident by early adulthood and often start with masochistic or sadistic play in childhood. The disorder is characterized by intense sexually arousing fantasies, urges, or behaviors in which the individual is sexually aroused by causing humiliation or physical suffering of another person. There are different theories related to sexual sadism, many stemming from the psychoanalytic camp. They suggest that childhood trauma (e.g., sexual abuse) or significant childhood experiences can manifest in exhibitionistic behavior.

- *Transvestic fetishism:* This diagnosis is used for heterosexual males who have sexually arousing fantasies, urges, or behaviors involving cross-dressing (wearing female clothing). To be considered diagnosable, the fantasies, urges, or behaviors must cause significant distress in the individual or be disruptive to his or her everyday functioning. There are different theories related to this disorder, many stemming from the psychoanalytic camp. They suggest that childhood trauma (e.g., sexual abuse or other significant sexual experience) or significant childhood experiences can manifest in exhibitionistic behavior.

- *Voyeurism:* This disorder is characterized by intense sexually arousing fantasies, urges, or behaviors in which the individual observes an unsuspecting stranger who is naked, disrobing, or engaging in sexual activity. To be considered diagnosable, the fantasies, urges, or behaviors must cause significant distress in the individual or be disruptive to his or her everyday functioning. There are different theories related to exhibitionistic behaviors, many stemming from the psychoanalytic camp. They suggest that childhood trauma (e.g., sexual abuse) or significant childhood experiences can manifest in exhibitionistic behavior.

People with these addictions may act out their desires in many ways. Some secretly cross-dress, spy on others in what they consider provocative situations, buy pornography, or seek gratification on the Internet. Others seek prostitutes or extramarital affairs to satisfy their urges. All of these are especially true of ministers, who need to hide their addictions from their spouses and especially the public. Others act out more destructively through sexual assault, molestation, or rape. If sex is not forced, the perpetrator attempts to persuade his victim to engage in sexual acts that are consistent with the desires driven by his addiction. He may ask his victims to engage in role play, beat them, request to be beaten, or force them to have their picture taken or be videoed in erotic poses.

These addictions are treatable if care from a therapy professional is sought. For example, sexual fetishes are typically treated with psychotherapy aimed at uncovering and resolving the underlying cause of the behavior. However, therein is the issue with mega-church leaders. They are among the primary types of people with addictions who are not likely to seek treatment because of embarrassment, pride, and fear of being publicly exposed. However, failure to seek treatment often becomes their downfall. Adults who are attracted to children provide an example.

Joe Barron was one of about 40 ministers of the 26,000-member Prestonwood Baptist Church in Plano, Texas. He was arrested in May 2008 after driving three hours from the Dallas, Texas, area to Bryan, Texas, seeking sex with who he thought was a 13-year-old girl he had met on the Internet. Instead, he had been communicating with an undercover law enforcement officer. He was jailed for a second time after being charged with four new complaints of online solicitation of a minor.

In a similar case not involving a mega-church leader but also a minister who exemplifies sexual addiction, Gordon Solomon, pastor at Christ's Community Church of Los Angeles in Inglewood, California, was charged in July 2012 with having a two-year sexual relationship with a 14-year-old girl. The news of his acts both shocked and devastated the members of his church. According to the Los Angeles Sheriff's Department, the two exchanged emails and texts of a sexual nature as well as met at various locations. The victim's mother stumbled upon an inappropriate text sent to the girl and immediately called the police. The married 50-year-old minister was charged with seven felony counts of committing a lewd act on a child, one felony count of oral copulation of a person under the age of 14, and one felony count of continuous sexual abuse. He was placed on $3 million bail, and authorities reported they have reason to believe there may be other victims. Reportedly, as a leader of the church, Solomon worked alongside children during Bible classes, computer lessons, and choir rehearsals.

Sexual addictions originate for many reasons. Some start due to experiences from childhood. In *Healing the Wounds of Sexual Addiction*, Laaser describes this as "imprinting." He states, "When adults continue to act out what was imprinted on them as children, they may be returning to their original feelings of sexual excitement. The concept of imprinting is an important one for anyone who works with adolescents and teens. Having sexual experiences before marriage has potent and long-lasting effects. One's first sexual experience is very powerful and should be reserved for marriage. When this kind of repetition occurs, it perpetuates the cycle of sexual abuse."[25]

Some addicts were abused by a parent, sibling, other relative, or someone not related to them. This can have a lifelong impact, leading to the inability to understand normal sexual behavior, the inability to maintain stable monogamous relationships, or the inability to ever maintain a healthy sexual relationship. In some, for example, it can lead to fear of sexual contact. Others may have had an overly intimate relationship with their parents. This does not mean they were molested nor that they had sexually intimate contact with a parent. However, they may have been exposed to situations during which they regularly witnessed their parents in sexual situations or were exposed to sexual images or situations that resulted in psychological damage. Conversely, some may have been deprived of normal parental intimacy. This includes outright rejection or being denied physical contact or emotional support. Being socially deprived of affection and attention can permanently damage a person's self-esteem. Another factor leading to sexual addiction or deviancy is abuse. Physical and mental abuse damages a person's self-esteem and leads to hostile behavior through adulthood. This hostility may be taken out on others of the same or different sex through sexual behavior meant to damage the victim mentally or physically.

Acts considered sexually addictive in one country or locality, however, may seem normal in others. Sociocultural factors contribute to and determine acts deemed sexually appropriate. This is because some actions deemed acceptable in one culture are not deemed so in others. For example, in some countries prostitution, having sex with minors, or sexual promiscuity by married men is legal and/or culturally acceptable. People from or heavily influenced by these cultures may face social scrutiny or criminal prosecution in other localities. Consider cases discussed by Ahn and Gilbert in their 1992 article entitled "Cultural Diversity and Sexual Abuse Prevention" in *Social Services Review* about foreigners living in the United States. Two Filipino nannies were accused of sexual abuse because they fondled and masturbated children they were caring for. The women claimed this was an acceptable practice in the Philippines. A Korean man was accused of sexual abuse for touching the genitals of a young boy. In his Korean culture, this is an expression of adoration and pride for a male child who is expected to carry on the family name and tradition. A Vietnamese man was accused of sexual abuse for the same act against a male child. In his culture, this was regarded as an expression of fondness. However, people are expected to abide by the laws and cultural norms of the country, state, or locality in which they are citizens or live. In the case of the Vietnamese man discussed earlier, he did not face any criminal charges but had to undergo therapy to learn that he was expected to respect his son's rights and privacy because he was living in the United States. The man found this difficult to understand, given that children were taught to respect their parents in his country. This respect meant they did not question their parents and they certainly did not have the right to private space as Americans view it.

Many people find it difficult to adapt to local laws and cultures. It may take years to fully assimilate and fully understand why behaviors thought normal for most of one's life are now considered odd, immoral, or illegal. Many also have no frame of reference to think their behavior is wrong when engaging in such private family issues as cobathing, cosleeping, and displaying parental affection in front of their children through such acts as kissing.

The majority of people with sexual addictions struggle with them for most or all of their lives. Some seek professional treatments and are able to cope with them. Others remain silent. Those who do not seek professional support can find it hard to maintain normal lives and healthy relationships. Those in the ministry often struggle with sexual addictions in silence. However, they are tempted not only by what can be characterized as the "ample supply" of potential victims churches offer because they wield so much power, but also because they work in an environment where the church typically is slow to respond when sexual abuse occurs. As Grenz and Bell point out in *Betrayal of Trust: Confronting and Preventing Clergy Sexual Misconduct*, "Clergy sexual misconduct takes many forms, including exhibitionism, voyeurism, child molestation, incest, homosexual promiscuity, and rape. In fact, ministers are exempted from no type of aberrant sexual behavior. Often a pastor finds himself waging a long, lonely battle against the temptation to engage in conduct he knows is unacceptable and dangerous. Sometimes, however, a minister not only loses the battle but even draws the church into his destructive conduct as the congregation becomes the source for the victim of his self-gratification."[26] Congregations feed this behavior in mega-churches because they allow their leader to have so much authority and power over the church. Often rumors or even known indiscretions are dismissed. What is worse is those in the congregation who know the issues to be true but feel their leader is justified because either they have the same type of addiction, or feel the minister is owed that much because of what he has and continues to do for the church. As is shown in cases throughout this book, there is often a culture of maintaining church secrets within the church. This includes the church paying off victims and then threatening them so that they will remain silent. This issue of the church's role in mega-church sexual misconduct will be discussed in detail in Chapter 4.

Various psychological factors beyond sexual addiction may lead to sexual misconduct. Midlife crisis issues are a factor to consider. Men going through midlife crises, for example, are prone to engage in extramarital affairs. Feeling the end of their ability to attract younger women (or men), they engage in affairs as a method to boost their self-esteem as they cope with the fear of aging. As written by Brehony in *Awakening at Midlife*, at midlife, "the underlying, often unconscious psychological issues that are straining to emerge, the search for wholeness that occurs at this time, and the frequent confrontation of one's own and other's mortality are not so simple, nor are they restricted by gender, class, education, or any other demographic variable. The midlife transition is a deeply human experience. Some of us may drift into it unconsciously, barely noticing the effects, while others of us will feel as if we've been knocked over the head with a two-by-four."[27] Psychologist Carl Jung is credited with first identifying the concept of midlife crisis and then discussing the difficulties of giving up one's image of youth while at the same time accepting mortality. He explored the concept of individuation as he was dealing with his own midlife issues that were affecting his creativity, emerging from the experience with a renewed sense of his inner self.[28]

Many people find it difficult to deal with graying hair or balding, weight gain, a reduction in sexual urges, and other bodily changes that occur at midlife. All of these impact self-esteem and the feeling of being attractive to others. Along with the desire to recapture the feelings of youth by engaging in sexual affairs, affairs also result from feeling discontent with the progress made in one's life, being bored with one's current situation (including one's marriage and role as parent), the need for excitement, and confusion about where one's life is going. The period of midlife, beginning at approximately 40 years of age, is also difficult due to factors aside from aging. It is during this period that many people begin dealing with ailing or dying parents and friends, debt, and other demands that impact their stress levels.

Given the average age of mega-church leaders, many are engaging in sexual misconduct due to the psychological effects of midlife and the combination of other contributing factors such as wealth and power. To deal with their mental struggles with life, they have the financial resources to take advantage of whatever fantasies or wants they desire. Cheating is not uncommon for men and women going through midlife issues because they often take their frustrations out on their spouses and partners. According to Wexler in *When Good Men Behave Badly: Change Your Behavior, Change Your Relationship*, "Both men and women often project the blame for their unhappiness and lack of fulfillment on their most intimate partner, even when these feelings are triggered by other pressures like raising children, caring for aging and dying parents, work stresses and disappointments, aging bodies and the loss of self-esteem, fears of mortality, or the tediousness of family life. They can become lost in dark moods, enveloped in an impenetrable fog of blame that distorts the view of the other."[29]

At the same time the minister is going through midlife, so may his wife. This complicates the situation even more. They both may be suffering with anxiety, depression, and questions about their marriage. At midlife, a woman often begins dealing with hormonal changes such as hot flashes, eating disorders, and selfish behaviors. Men at midlife sometimes develop destructive coping mechanisms such as costly infatuations, alcoholism, or addiction to work. They also both must adjust to being in the home alone for the first time in decades as their adult children leave the home, commonly called the empty nest syndrome. In general, studies find that issues related to values, communication, commitment, decision making, emotional intimacy, and sexuality are the most common causes of problems for married couples during midlife. The stress and responsibilities of being a mega-church minister may add to the difficulties of coping with these issues unless counseling is sought. Both individual and marriage counseling may be required.

JOB STRESS

Stress and burnout are common problems among ministers. Approximately 1,500 pasters lave the ministry each year. Another fifty percent would leave if they could afford it.[30] Ministers have demanding jobs. They are the spiritual leaders of hundreds, or in the case of mega-church leaders, thousands. The amount of time spent giving sermons, meeting with members, counseling, speaking publicly, and dealing with church business can be exhausting and sometimes overwhelming. In *Ministry Burnout*, Sanford outlines some of the factors that make ministers' jobs so stressful:[31]

- The minister's job is never finished.
- The minister cannot always tell if his work is having any results.
- The minister's work is repetitive.
- The minister is dealing constantly with people's expectations.
- The minister must work with the same people year in and year out.
- Because he works with people in need, there is a particularly great drain on the minister's energy.
- The minister deals with many people who come to him or the church not for solid spiritual food but for "strokes."
- The minister may become exhausted by failure.

Ministers also face what has been called the Sisyphus complex. In Greek mythology, Sisyphus was a mythological king who was cursed to roll a huge boulder up a hill, only to watch it roll down again, and to repeat rolling the boulder back up the hill throughout eternity. The work of ministers is analogous to the trials of Sisyphus. Ministers must give sermons each week, visit sick members, provide counseling, and repetitively perform an array of other duties. They may sometimes feel they are performing the same tasks over and over while not really making progress because they constantly engage in the same types of actions and deal with the same types of issues. One can imagine the impact this has on a mega-church minister who is leading so many. Stress from work affects personal lives, often leading to stress at home. Spouses may try to provide comfort but are shunned because the minister feels emotionally isolated in thinking his spouse cannot truly understand or appreciate his stress. The marriage can worsen if the minister's feelings of being overwhelmed lead to anxiety or depression.

These factors lead to disillusionment. As Grosch and Olsen further explain in the *Journal of Clinical Psychology*, "Disillusionment sets in for some as their initial optimism and enthusiasm fades. This disillusionment can manifest itself in a variety of ways, ranging from boredom, to cynicism towards parishioners, to anger at committee meetings, to simply dragging through the day. They continue to go through the motions, but the joy is gone. Many report feeling that their spiritual well is completely dry. Others reach the extreme of total burnout and breakdown; some even resort to sexual misconduct, leading to ruined careers."[32]

Occupational stress is especially acute for mega-church leaders. They must first balance the responsibilities of leading thousands of members, and without the same support structure as ministers in organized religions. This creates an extreme demand on their time beyond delivering sermons. Many members want personal interaction so that they can talk about their faith, personal problems, recommendations to improve the church, and other issues. There is constant pressure to maintain the same or higher number of members to the meet the increasing monetary demands of the church as it grows. At the same time, ministers have to oversee a staff of hundreds, ensuring they are properly performing their duties. They are also responsible for overseeing budgets of millions of dollars. These tremendous management, human resource, and fiscal responsibilities are equivalent to the demands of chief executive officers (CEOs) and chief investment officers (CIOs) of major corporations. However, ministers are not trained in human resource management and finance. In most churches, neither are their senior staff members.

Church leaders must also balance demands external to the church. This includes responding to the media, community leaders and groups, government agencies, other religious entities, and church nonmembers personally requesting consultation. All of these tasks must be undertaken while the ministers are also extensively traveling, writing books, and even producing videos and movies. Most have no training in public relations, government relations, or capital investment. They learn as the church grows, and they gain experience through trial and error. In addition, they must balance the aforementioned responsibilities with their personal lives, including their personal health and interests in addition to family responsibilities.

All of these combined demands have the potential of creating extremely high stress levels and various coping mechanisms, including sexual misconduct. Studies have found the same results in people in other high stress occupations, including police officers and nurses. For example, an article in the *National Institute of Justice Journal* outlines the results of stress experienced by police officers. These include such marital or family problems as extramarital affairs, divorce, and domestic violence. Other effects are cynicism and suspicion, emotional detachment from daily life, reduced efficiency, excessive aggressiveness, and such health problems as heart attacks, ulcers, and weight gain.[33] It is easy to see how ministers of mega-churches would face the same or similar effects given the demands of their jobs.

People deal with stress in different ways, but sometimes with unhealthy behaviors. Some turn to food, others to alcohol and drugs, and others to sex. All of these can become vices used to escape from the realities of everyday life because they are seen as providing some form of temporary mental and physical escape. However, choosing destructive escape mechanisms lead to three negative outcomes in the case of sexual misconduct. The first is sexual addiction that requires a continuation or intensification of the misconduct in order to maintain the same or higher levels of stress reduction. Stress can either start or trigger an addictive cycle. The stress encountered at work then mimics the addictive cycle of sexual addiction. Just as work has periods of high stress and low stress, periods of acting upon the sexual addiction have periods of radical behavior that leads to the satisfaction of that behavior and then dissatisfaction, and then reverts to the need to engage in that behavior again. As Dr. Patrick J. Carnes explains in *Out of the Shadows: Understanding Sexual Addiction*, "The addiction is truly a system where behavior is interdependent. There are constantly shifting patterns that weave together the various levels of sexually compulsive behavior and that may include other addictions and emotional disorders. The system operates on a repetitive rhythm. The driving force for each cycle comes from a faulty belief system translated through delusional thought patterns. In general, systems are self-perpetuating, and the sexual addition as a system is just that. The completion of each cycle confirms that belief system and a new and stronger cycle is born."[34] For church leaders, this may lead to the desire to engage in sex with different people in order to satisfy their recurring desires.

The second negative outcome of choosing destructive coping mechanisms is the negative impact on those the minister is involved with and a growing loss of concern about their feelings. The culprit may not even care about feelings of pleasure or sensation in the other person; rather, the minister may care only about his own desire for stress relief. To fulfill his sexual needs, the minister carefully plans how, where, and when he will act upon his desires. In most cases, ministers engaging in sexual misconduct know what they are thinking is wrong, and there is a period of feeling shame, guilt, and apprehension. However, their urges and impulses overcome any feelings of remorse, and eventually they find a way to engage in their desired behavior again. In *Healing the Wounds of Sexual Addiction*, Laaser describes this process as beginning with constant thoughts of sex, then a cycle of hoped-for sexual activities without regard for moral or spiritual boundaries, followed by a cycle of guilt and shame but then repeating the sin. However, the culprit justifies the sexual misconduct as a means to cope with stress and work demands. During this process, depression and shame over what has been done may also lead a minister to engage in sex to find some level of temporary happiness. Until a perpetrator gets help to stop the behavior, this cycle will continue.[35]

The third negative outcome of ministers choosing destructive coping mechanisms is the same as for others who engage in sexual misconduct in the workplace. Since in this case misconduct is being conducted by a mega-church leader and the minister always represents the church, this misconduct is taking place in the workplace—the church—whether the actions take place on or off church property. This creates an environment of tension for church members and staff, animosity, loss of morale, and loss of respect for the church leader and all others directly and indirectly involved. In nonchurch workplaces, a similar situation may lead to personnel quitting or taking positions in other parts of the company. In churches, sexual misconduct and the subsequent tension lead to members and staff leaving the church. Other impacts to the church are the same as in businesses, schools, governments, and any other setting. These include loss of financial resources, damage to self-esteem, loss of productivity, loss of money, absenteeism, member isolation, and illness from stress.

Ministers must develop healthy mechanisms to deal with stress. This includes taking vacations, balancing family and work life, learning how to delegate tasks to subordinates, and realizing personal limitations when dealing with a diverse group of members with so many different types of needs and problems. They must also take comfort and turn to the very faith they represent to their members. Just as other people do, ministers get overwhelmed with their jobs and can become depressed. They too are susceptible to developing negative coping mechanisms such as overeating, abusing alcohol or drugs, or engaging in sexual misconduct. They have to learn to practice the basics of stress relief, including learning how to relax, eating well, and getting plenty of exercise. They also must seek professional counseling when needed.

TEMPTATION, DECEPTION, AND ACCOUNTABILITY

Up until this point, this chapter has examined the reasons mega-church leaders engage in acts of sexual misconduct. However, the primary question is at what point do their actions begin? At what point do their innate sexual desires or temptations overtake their moral and spiritual responsibility? Unfortunately, it seems the answer is that their acts of misconduct parallel their churches' level of success. When these churches are founded, they have small memberships and the church leader is under scrutiny. As the church grows so do leaders' popularity, power, and propensity to adopt more secular behavior. At the same time, their egos grow, making them feel more invincible in terms of scrutiny and freedom to take liberties. The same is true of other leaders. President Bill Clinton allegedly had affairs before becoming president. As governor of Arkansas, he allegedly involved state police officers in his sexual escapades. As president, he was so bold as to commit sexual acts with an intern in the Oval Office of the White House.

Lammers, Stapel, and Galinsky conducted a study to determine if power increases moral hypocrisy, a situation characterized by imposing strict moral standards on others but practicing less strict moral behavior oneself. In an article in *Psychological Science*, they reported that "the powerful impose more normative restraints on others, but believe they themselves can act with less restraint. The less powerful, in contrast, are less inclined to impose norms on others, but more rigidly follow these themselves. This means that people with power not only take what they want because they can do so unpunished, but also because they intuitively feel they are entitled to do so." Their study also found that "if the powerful sense that their unrestrained self-enrichment leads to gossiping, derision, and the undermining of their reputation as conscientious leaders, then they may be inspired to bring their behavior back to their espoused standards. If they fail to do so, they may quickly lose their authority, reputation, and—eventually—their power."[36] This study applies directly to mega-church leaders. They preach issues of morality and condemn the behavior of others, yet some do not feel that this same level of morality applies to them. Eddie Long is but one example. A 2007 article in the Southern Poverty Law Center's magazine *Intelligence Report* called him "one of the most virulently homophobic black leaders in the religiously based anti-gay movement."[37] Long was so vigilant in his attacks on homosexuals that the funeral of Coretta Scott King in his church in 2006 was protested by many, including actor Harry Belafonte and Julian Bond, then chairperson of the National Association for the Advancement of Colored People (NAACP). Bond publicly stated, "I knew her [Coretta Scott King's] attitude toward gay and lesbian rights. I just couldn't imagine that she'd want to be in that church with a minister who was a raving homophobe."[38] While Long launched a religious battle against homosexuals, he engaged in sex with at least four adolescent boys on repeated occasions.

Power, innate sexual desires, temptation, and stress explain why some mega-church leaders commit acts of sexual misconduct. However, there is a level of sexual addiction that also drives their behavior that is evident in the many who repetitively engage in acts. Pastor Jeff Fisher was once addicted to pornography and spoke in an article in *The Christian Post* about how ministers may be more vulnerable to sexual temptation than others. He stated that

no one is immune to sexual temptation. It doesn't matter what your job is, how old you are, or how much time you spend with Jesus each day. We all have the potential to fall sexually. Even ministers ... and maybe, especially ministers. Ministers have jobs that automatically put them in a pressure cooker ... Isolation with no accountability is a prelude to disaster. When we cut ourselves off from others we're shutting off sources of truth and objectivity. We lose the opportunity for fellowship and confession ... Accountability can be personal ... other men asking you key questions. But it can also take the form of church policies. If I have good policies for my visitation and counseling they can help me establish boundaries. If the policies around the pastorate are regularly reviewed, that can be a good measure of protection for the minister. If you have accountability, software on your personal laptop and on the church computers, it provides another level of transparency that is essential for maintaining sexual purity.[39]

Mega-church leaders who engage in sexual, financial or legal misconduct are betraying their faith, families, congregations, and all that their religion it is supposed to represent: devotion, fortitude, commitment, love, spirituality, and virtue. Horst provides an accurate description of the situation in *Questions and Answers about Clergy Misconduct*:

Sex between people who are not married to each other (unchastity) or sex with person A when you are married to person B (adultery) may violate community standards, but trying to figure out which sexual sin has been committed may be a wild goose chase in the specific case of sexual misconduct by clergy. The relevant issue here is not, or at least not only, sex outside of marriage, but sex across a gap in power. If you cheat on your marriage vows by getting sexually involved with your next door neighbor, you have betrayed the trust of your spouse. If you are a pastor and you become sexually involved with a congregant, you have also betrayed the trust of the entire congregation, damaged the spiritual life of the people you are called to serve, risked the financial and administrative security of your church or faith community, and most likely taken advantage of someone entrusted to your care. A cleric having sex with a teenage in the youth group or with a counselee in the church office is doing harm, not primarily because the behavior is sexual, but because it is coercive.[40]

Horst raises two important points. First, ministers are charged with the spiritual and personal care of their congregants. They are responsible for delivering teachings and lessons that help guide their members to spiritual and mental happiness. More than being assigned as a job duty, it is a moral and religious responsibility the minister assumes as head of the church. Those that violate this responsibility are betraying a trust that is deemed by society to be one of the most sacred. It is a violation of one of the basic principles of trust in almost every culture. Second, the sexual act is coercive by the mere fact the act is between a congregant and his or her minister. As Horst further states,

> Clergy are often unaware of the amount of influence they have, but congregants generally grant them a level of authority that makes their words and actions automatically credible. It's a lot harder to put the brakes on a sexual encounter initiated by a beloved and trusted pastor, or to figure out how to avoid unwelcome touch by the priest your parents taught you to respect and obey, than it is to turn down, say, a lewd invitation from a drunk in a bar. Offending clergy take advantage, sometimes unconsciously but nonetheless intentionally, of the position of privilege granted them by the community and the larger Church. As soon as a clergy is involved in a sexual relationship, s/he is no longer maintaining the role of professional helper. Offending clergy violate their responsibility to look out for the best interests of those in their care.[41]

This lack of responsibility and coerciveness applies even if the minister engages in sexual misconduct with someone from outside of the church. Church leaders gain inherent respect in their positions by the community and by general members of society. When one takes on the role of representing and spreading the words of his religion, it is inherent that this responsibility applies to every aspect of one's life, within and outside of the church. In this respect, a minister is like congressional representatives. Even when they leave the building, they conduct business; they represent the people 24 hours a day, seven days a week. They are expected to engage in ethically and legally acceptable behavior at all times.

The decision to lead so many involves the decision to commit oneself to the very edicts one espouses in messages based upon the most basic tenants of one's religion. Mega-church leaders have a level of accountability that not only exists in their actions within the church, but also in their daily lives. As Elisha discusses in *Moral Ambition: Mobilization and Social Outreach in Evangelical Megachurches*, "Accountability functions among evangelicals as a theological and instructional paradigm that is applicable to every aspect of their life, from how they run their homes and businesses to matters of sexual morality and family life to even broader notions of religious, civic, and political responsibility ... As an organizational principle, the concept of accountability helps to legitimize the authority of church pastors and elders, especially in mega-churches with large budgets and influence."[42] Personal accountability for acts of sexual misconduct applies not only to the church leader, but also to those under his charge. Cordova, Tennessee's Bellevue Baptist Church Pastor Steve Gaines is an example. In 2006, a minister on his staff, Paul Williams, admitted to having molested a child some years earlier. Williams had served at the church for 34 years, and he made the admission of his acts to Gaines in confidence. Gaines reported nothing to the authorities, although Tennessee law requires that "Any person who has knowledge of or is called upon to render aid to any child who is suffering from or has sustained any wound, injury, disability, or physical or mental condition shall report such harm immediately if the harm is of such a nature as to reasonably indicate that it has been caused by brutality, abuse or neglect or that, on the basis of available information, reasonably appears to have been caused by brutality, abuse or neglect" (Tennessee code Section 37-1-403). Gaines announced the incident ambiguously to the church six months after Williams was placed on paid leave pending a church investigation. Allegedly, the child Williams molested was his own son over a period of 12 to 18 months. Beyond Gaines, at least 10 others affiliated with the church knew about the abuse prior to it being publicly announced, including family members.

In a statement, Gaines said, "Some people have questioned why I waited for several months. It's simply this: I acted out of a heartfelt concern and compassion for this minister because the event occurred many years ago, he was receiving professional counseling, and I was concerned about confidentiality. In light of the events that have unfolded, I realize now that I should have discussed it further with this minister and brought it to the attention of our church leadership immediately."[43] The church fired Williams after it conducted its own investigation.

The question from this case and those similar to it is if the decision to wait on taking action against the perpetrator is really in the best interest of the church. Or is it a tactic to protect the minister and the church? Or perhaps it is just a tactic to wait and see if the issue will simply go away. In examples provided throughout this book, it is clear how mega-churches may attempt act as businesses but in essence are not. Businesses have clearly established rules for how acts of sexual harassment and sexual abuse will be handled. These rules and policies are put in place to protect businesses from lawsuits. Churches can also be sued and the actions of their leaders punished by law. However, proving wrongful acts took place seems much more difficult in the context of churches. This is predominantly so because churches act under a banner of religion, and their inner operations are shielded from public knowledge and thus scrutiny. Law enforcement officials have to rely on members of the church collaborating with their investigations, which is often difficult. For this reason, there is not only accountability for the minister to act in the best interest of the church, but also accountability by church staff and members to act in the best interest of the community and society when the leader does commit criminal acts. This is a complex issue for churches that view their church and religious laws as outweighing those of society. For example, adultery and jealousy are not laws punishable by society, but they are considered moral sins in the church. Societal laws are not forgiving;

rather, they prescribe a range of punishments when a person is convicted based on the level and scope of the crime. Religions preach forgiveness of even for the most heinous crimes.

The lack of accountability in cases of sexual misconduct sometimes ends in tragedy for ministers and for those they engage in sex with. Zachery Tims was pastor of the 7,500-member New Destiny Church in Apopka, Florida. He founded the church in 1996 with only six members. He was found dead in a New York City hotel in 2011 at the age of 42. While the details of his death have not been fully revealed because of a court order instigated by his family, a white substance was found in his pocket that was alleged to be a controlled substance. In 2009, he and his wife filed for divorce after he admitted to having an affair with a stripper he met in Paris, France. One of Eddie Long's victims reported the minister attempted suicide weeks after the sexual lawsuits against Long were filed. The victim, Centino Kemp, reported he had been sexually and physically abused by Long for six years. During an interview with Oprah Winfrey in 2009, Ted Haggard revealed he considered suicide after his sexual relationship with a male prostitute was made public.

Leader accountability does not just mean preaching a message based on theology. It entails living a life in public and private that exemplifies the tenants members of the congregation are expected to follow. This is not a philosophical notion but a fact based upon the role mega-church leaders assume as head of their churches. Those that violate the trust of accountability in their positions should voluntarily remove themselves from their positions or be forcibly removed. What is troubling about mega-church leaders who commit acts of sexual misconduct is that they preach the moral sins and unforgivable behavior of others while they commit the same or worse acts. Those who espouse hatred of homosexuality are an example. Their message sometimes leads to hatred by followers, and feelings of depression and suicide in those that are targeted. Some of these ministers then privately engage in the same behavior, using religion as a shield.

Some argue that ministers are only human and thus are susceptible to succumbing to the same temptation as other people do. Although they are men of the cloth, they are in the end flesh and blood and as such are subject to the same failings as "normal" men and women. While this may be true, some mega-church leaders commit acts of sexual misconduct over and over rather than falling to temptation a single time. They have multiple affairs, purposely hide their behavior for years, and then becry their human failings only after their acts of discretion are publicly revealed. Some people feel that these are not the actions of a person who simply cannot resist an act of physical temptation, but rather the actions of a habitual sexual liar. Earl Paulk is an example. He founded the Chapel Hill Harvester Church in Decatur, Georgia, and served as its pastor from 1960 until the late 1990s. Several women claimed that Paulk had sex with them, and he was also accused of child molestation. His supposed nephew, Donnie Earl Paulk, had a court-ordered DNA test performed when he was in his 30s and serving as senior pastor of the church. The test revealed Earl Paulk was not his uncle, but rather his father. This revealed that Earl Paulk was also having an affair with his brother's wife.

The issue with ministers is that more is expected of them in terms of resisting temptation. This is one of the primary messages of their sermons to their congregations. There are expectations of personal and professional boundaries ministers will maintain with their congregation members, those they are counseling, and those they come in contact with while conducting church business. These same boundaries are expected of ministers in their personal lives, particularly when they are married. Ministers must maintain many boundaries, not only resist temptation. These include not compromising their beliefs (theological boundaries), not violating the trust of those the counsel (ethical and professional boundaries), not abusing church funds (economic boundaries), and attending to the various needs of their families (family boundaries). The same professional boundaries expected of ministers are expected of doctors, lawyers, and teachers as they serve the needs of their clients, whether they be church members, students, or patients. The duty of these professionals is to meet the needs of those they serve, not their own.

The issue of personal accountability, or the lack thereof, by some church leaders has been best explained by Dr. Ben Witherington, a professor at Ashbury Theological Seminary. He often blogs on religious issues. His posting on November 3, 2006 came after Ted Haggard stepped down as head of the 14,000-member Evangelical Church and the National Association of Evangelicals after it was revealed he had had a three-year relationship with a male prostitute. According to Witherington, mega-church leaders commit such acts for the following reason that are common in evangelical mega-churches:[44]

Most of these large churches are not part of denominations which have a connectional enough system to hold the individual church leadership accountable through peer leaders in other churches. By this I mean there is little outside accountability. There are no covenant relationships with other church leaders, no covenant relationships with other churches, the leadership structure is entirely controlled INTERNALLY between influential lay persons and the ministers.

He goes on to explain how the power and isolation of mega-churches are concentrated with their leaders. This cult-like structure leads to abuses of power, including sexual misconduct. This abuse of power is coupled with other issues leader are facing such as midlife crises, job stress, and an overall lack of accountability due to noone verifying they are behaving in the best interest of the church.

MARITAL PROBLEMS

Just as normal married couples do, mega-church leaders have marital issues. These issues may lead them to cheat. Noted psychotherapist and counselor Gary Neuman studied the primary reasons men cheat. In *The Truth about Cheating: Why Men Stray and What You Can Do to Prevent It*, he discussed his finding that the majority of husbands (48%) reported emotional dissatisfaction in their marriage as the primary reason. Other reasons were equal emotional and sexual dissatisfaction (32%), other/no dissatisfaction (12%), and primarily sexual dissatisfaction (8%). Overall, 59 percent responded the reason there was dissatisfaction in their marriages was emotional, 29 percent that their dissatisfaction was sexual, and 12 percent that it was for other reasons.[45]

Ministerial couples argue about money, fall out of love, have sexual problems stemming from the husband or wife, and may reach a point in their marriage where they are just not happy with each other anymore. All of these factors may lead couples to split, but it is more difficult for a minister of a mega-church and his wife to separate or divorce because of their positions in the church and the community (in some cases within the country). A mega-church leader and his wife are held to a high standard of representing the perfect married couple to thousands of other married couples. If they separate or divorce, many in the church will question their devotion and faith in comparison to the lessons the minister has been teaching. There will also be questions and rumors related to the reasons the couple split, with questions of infidelity at the top of the list. Accusations of infidelity will mainly be directed toward the minister.

Stress and turmoil in marriages often cause one or both spouses to seek outside companionship and sex. Because the marriage has become an institution within the church and the community, the minister does not seek divorce for fear of how others will react and what they will think and say. At the same time, his marriage has become a part of his life. This includes becoming a major part of his appeal and image as a minister. Parallel to this is the need to obtain sexual gratification from somewhere.

Sometimes, an affair begins with a simple friendship that develops when the minister finds someone with whom he is comfortable talking about his marital problems. Over time, the friendship develops into a relationship as each begins to confide in the other about individual problems. In other cases, sex is the primary driver for starting the relationship. As discussed earlier, men going through midlife crises who respond by engaging in extramarital affairs create serious problems for their families, the person they are having an affair with, and possibly their community. As young men, they may have slept with others as part of sexual experimentation. As middle-aged adults, they are socially, economically, and physically wise to their actions and capabilities. They are aware of how to manipulate others to get what they want. However, they may care little about whom they hurt in the process. They may not be concerned about their families and their responsibilities related to taking care of them. They may not be concerned about whether their affair partner is married. They may also be willing to risk close relationships, their jobs, and even their financial futures to satisfy their current desires.

It is understandable that there may be marital stress between a mega-church minister and his spouse that may exist for years. The couple faces financial and time pressures when their church is first beginning, given these churches begin with few members, and ministers spend enormous amounts of time trying to grow their churches. Beginning the church may require the minister to quit his secular job, move his family across country to a desired church location, and spend a large amount of time away from home. His wife may be forced into being the primary financial supporter of the family while the church struggles to grow. Additionally, the wife may not have really wanted to be the wife of a practicing minister. She may not be prepared for how much of her time and personal interests she has to give up, nor may she be prepared for the scrutiny from church members and the community. As the "first lady" of the church, she is expected to be the role model of the perfect wife and mother. There is also the isolation inherent in being the church leader's wife. This isolation results from the difficulty in making close friends with female or male members of the church.

She may not also want to live in an urban area, but that is where most mega-churches are located. This is especially true of women who grew up in small towns or those who just do not want to raise their children in an urban environment. As the church grows, ministers are away from home and spend time meeting with new members and community groups, as well as performing other activities that keep them away from home. The wife may find herself at times assuming all the responsibilities of maintaining the home and raising the children.

The minister and spouse are both then exposed to a new reality of growing success they were not prepared for. As the church explodes in popularity (as mega-churches do within a few years of being established), neither the minister nor his wife may be prepared for the trials that come with wealth and fame. These include demands on their time, invasion of their private lives, constant scrutiny by the church and community, and extreme media attention. The success that comes with becoming the leader of a mega-church may lead to the primary reasons that ministerial couples face problems within their marriages. These include lack of communication, questioning if they are with the right person, and wondering if their spouse really supports their occupational, mental and physical needs. This is complicated by the realization that they can now have their choice of so many other people. All of this is on top of having to raise a family and children going through the normal trials of adolescence.

According the Center for Ministerial Care,

Surveys taken among ministers in recent years reveal troubling trends which have developed in ministerial marriages and families. In one study, over 80 percent of the pastors surveyed believed that pastoral ministry negatively affected their family. Of that same group, 33 percent said that being in ministry was an outright hazard to their family. In their interviews with several hundred ministerial couples, Emerge Ministries compiled the following statistics: 66 percent felt there was a problem with understanding between spouses, 58 percent said there was an emotional problem with either a child or a spouse, 54 percent had sexual problems in their relationship, and 49 percent admitted that they argued on a regular basis.[46]

The center further reported that "One of the major reasons for the additional stress connected with ministry is perception of always being on display, what is known as the 'fish bowl' or 'glass house' syndrome." As a result, thousands of ministers leave their churches each year. With their departure from the church, they or their spouse may also end their marriage.

Chapter 3

No Crimes Are Victimless: Who Are Mega-Church Leaders Committing Sexual Misconduct With?

The victims of mega-church leaders' sexual misconduct have included mistresses, same-sex partners, prostitutes of both sexes, and minors. In some cases, these were sexual assault victims and in others willing sexual partners. All of these were not victims from the standpoint of being raped or molested. However, they were all victims in terms of being sexually involved with a mega-church leader who was married, kept their relationship a secret, or somehow was part of a deceitful act that supported the leader's personal gratification over faith and dedication to the church. The reasons for getting sexually involved with the leader are varied. They range from fear, to being swayed by the leader's power, to seeking financial reciprocity. In some cases, it is the combination of all of these factors. The alleged victims of Eddie Long provide an example. Each of the four young men who accused Long of molesting them had similar accounts of their experiences. Long gave them money, cars, and other gifts in addition to placing them on the church's payroll. The young men were swayed by his power as leader of the church. They were also fearful of rejecting his advances given his power, use of religious manipulation to urge them into sexual acts; in some cases, they feared for their safety. This latter issue was the case when Long took them on trips both within and outside the United States and the boys were required to sleep in his room. Being hundreds and sometimes thousands of miles from home, they were unable to physically escape for fear of being abandoned without any means to return home.

The factor that victims of any act of sexual misconduct have in common is the realization that what is being done to them or what they are doing is wrong. This applies to those who are willing participants as well as those that are taken advantage of. In both cases, they experience subsequent emotional and possible physical damage as a result of the incident(s). For those that are sexually assaulted, the following are possible physical or psychological effects:[1]

POSSIBLE PHYSICAL EFFECTS OF SEXUAL ASSAULT

- Pain
- Injuries
- Nausea
- Vomiting
- Headaches

POSSIBLE EMOTIONAL/PSYCHOLOGICAL EFFECTS OF SEXUAL ASSAULT

- Shock/denial
- Irritability/anger
- Depression
- Social withdrawal
- Numbing/apathy (detachment, loss of caring)
- Restricted affect (reduced ability to express emotions)
- Nightmares/flashbacks
- Difficulty concentrating
- Diminished interest in sex or other activities
- Loss of self-esteem
- Loss of security/trust in others
- Guilt/shame/embarrassment
- Impaired memory
- Loss of appetite
- Suicidal ideation (thoughts of suicide and death)

- Substance abuse
- Psychological disorders

POSSIBLE PHYSIOLOGICAL EFFECTS OF SEXUAL ASSAULT

- Hypervigilance (always being on guard)
- Insomnia
- Exaggerated startle response (jumpiness)
- Panic attacks
- Eating problems/disorders
- Self-mutilation (cutting, burning, or otherwise hurting oneself)
- Sexual dysfunction (not being able to perform sexual acts)
- Hyperarousal (exaggerated feelings/responses to stimuli)

Even those who consensually engage in sex with ministers suffer repercussions. These often include remorse, shame, depression, anxiety, fear, and embarrassment. Although these feelings are common in those who have any type of affair or wrongful sexual encounter, they are often more intense in those who engage in sex with a religious figure. The feelings of personal and spiritual betrayal can be intense and last for years. Some develop emotional and behavioral dysfunctions that manifest as the inability to maintain healthy relationships, criminal behavior, and drug and substance abuse. These tendencies occur both during and after incidents take place. These feelings are even more intense when the minister shuns the person and refuses to continue a relationship. The person feels isolated because he or she cannot talk to anyone about what happened out of fear of being ridiculed and out of fear of how the minister will react if he finds out.

Sexual abuse that occurs over long periods of time may even lead to the victim's dysfunctional dependence. Victims may feel ashamed but at the same time may become addicted to the attention. They feel special because they were chosen by the perpetrator, especially because he is a minister. They also may psychologically twist the abuse into a feeling of receiving affection they are lacking from their parents, spouse, or friends. Long periods of sex abuse create such damage to a person's self-esteem that he or she may withdraw from all others except the abuser. Friends and family may notice the change but are helpless to understand why it is happening or what to do. Perpetrators of sexual abuse take advantage of this dysfunctional dependence. To control victims emotionally and physically, perpetrators further manipulate them psychologically. Perpetrators persuade victims to feel that they cannot trust or depend on anyone else.

Members of the church often become sexually involved with ministers because of the intimate nature of the minister-congregant relationship. This is similar to affairs or sexual encounters initiated by doctors, lawyers, and teachers. Ministers have close and intimate contacts with some of their members, which sometimes lead to sexual encounters. This happens when they spend time alone during trips, private counseling sessions, or church projects for which they must work closely together. Some of these minister-congregant sexual encounters are unwanted; others are consensual. The consensual incidents often occur because a church member feels the minister listens and understands better than anyone else, even a spouse. This often leads to romantic feelings, much as a patient may have toward his or her psychiatrist. Then there is the allure of the minister: handsome, confident, well dressed, compassionate, and wealthy. For some women (and men), the minister is perceived as the perfect man and the ideal husband or partner. There is an ample supply of singe women (and men) who are sexually attracted to the minister and actively seek his private attention. Last, there is the desire to please the minister and ensure his personal needs are met. For some, this entails simply bringing him meals or offering to volunteer for his pet projects. For others, it is being willing to provide personal comfort and even sex.

Sex between ministers and members of their congregations is not uncommon. A survey conducted by Chaves and Garland that was published in the *Journal for the Scientific Study of Religion* revealed that 3.1 percent of women who attend religious services at least monthly reported having been the object of a sexual advance by a clergyperson or religious leader in their own congregation since turning 18; 2.2 percent of regularly attending women reported a sexual advance from a married leader that did not lead to an openly acknowledged relationship.[2] As discussed throughout this book, those who engage in consensual sexual encounters or victims of sexual abuse rarely reveal what happened.

Many ask why these victims (in either consensual or nonconsensual incidents) did not resist the minister or report the incident as soon as it occurred. It is a difficult decision to publicly reveal one has been a sexual victim of a minister. In general, people who have been victims of any type of sexual abuse may take years to reveal what happened to them, if they ever do at all. This is troubling given the following statistics about sexual abuse in the United States:[3]

- Every two minutes, someone in the United States is sexually assaulted, with a total of approximately 207,754 victims of sexual assault per year (of those 12 years or older).

- 54 percent of sexual assaults are not reported to police; 97 percent of rapists will never go to jail.
- Approximately two-thirds of assaults are committed by someone known to the victim; 38 percent of rapists are friends or acquaintances.
- 44 percent of sexual assault victims are under the age of 18 (15% are under 12); 80 percent are under 30.
- 1 out of every 6 U.S. women has been the victim of an attempted or completed rape in her lifetime (14.8% completed rape; 2.8% attempted rape).
- About 3 percent of American men (1 out of every 33) have experienced an attempted or completed rape in their lifetime.
- 93 percent of juvenile sexual assault victims know their attacker:
  - 34.2 percent of attackers were family members
  - 58.7 percent were acquaintances
  - Only 7 percent of the perpetrators were strangers to the victim

Most victims just do not want people to know what has happened to them. For those abused by ministers, it is much more difficult than for a person who has been assaulted by an ordinary person. One first has to examine the personal faith that has been placed in the minister, perhaps for years. Beyond the emotional and physical harm of the abuse is the spiritual pain. Revealing a wrongdoing may seem to be revealing the betrayal of one's faith and dedication to the church. At the same time, there is the disbelief that one's minister has betrayed his faith for personal gratification. For this reason, the victim may analyze what he or she did wrong to entice a minister to betray his faith. This may lead the victim to not report any wrongdoing if he or she has feelings that he or she had any part in encouraging the event.

The person questions his or her own religious fortitude and faith, examining how he or she could allow himself or herself to succumb to the temptation. This leads to remorse, self-pity, and shame in the inability to resist temptation and thus risk some type of spiritual damnation for the actions. The majority of both children and adults who are sexually abused by a minister also lose their faith. For some, they are able to regain their faith only after years of soul searching and sometimes counseling. Others spend years feeling confusion and emptiness due to their loss of faith. They also face the pain of losing their church, which to some had become a place of comfort and a way to deal with the stresses of daily life.

The greatest issue for victims is fear of what will happen if they reveal what has happened. Foremost, there is fear that they will be blamed for tempting the church's leader into engaging in such an act. The fear of being blamed is common in rape and molestation cases. It is the reason most cases go unreported. However, the fear is even greater when the culprit is the religious leader of thousands of people, well respected in his community, and in many cases respected nationwide. Even when victims feel they did nothing wrong to lead to the incident, the fear of revealing the incident to thousands of members and thousands or even millions or nonmembers seems unthinkable. Scrutiny by the church, media, and perhaps law enforcement officials causes many to remain silent. This scrutiny also comes from families and close friends, who may resent the attention. One factor that does prompt coming forward is another person who experienced the same or similar event coming forward first. This gives some the courage to reveal what happened to them because they no longer feel alone in their turmoil. However, even then they may be first collectively accused of falsely seeking retribution for personal financial gains.

While victims remain silent, the culprit may continue similar actions against others for years. For example, Bob Moorehead became the senior pastor of Overlake Christian Church in 1970. The church was founded in 1969 in Kirkland, Washington, and moved to Redmond, Washington, in 1997. Under Moorehead, the church's weekly attendance grew from a few hundred to over 6,000 by 1997. In July 1996, he was arrested and charged with indecent exposure in a public restroom in Daytona Beach, Florida. By 1998, it was revealed that he had sexually touched and fondled male members of the congregation for years, mostly during baptisms and wedding ceremonies in the 1970s. Seventeen men came forward with accusations, but no criminal charges were filed. The elders of the church first exonerated him of charges but then changed course and removed him in 1999 after they reported new evidence had emerged that led them to conclude he was guilty of the charges (even though he denied it). The elders sent a letter explaining their decision to church members. When the church moved to its new site in 1997, Rick Kingham was hired as senior pastor. He resigned after allegations of inappropriately using church funds. By 2007, the church's membership had dropped by half.[4]

Beyond the fear victims have of public and personal scrutiny is the fear of reprisal. Leaders of mega-churches are extremely wealthy, well connected, and charismatic. Their power is evidenced by their ability to persuade thousands to follow them religiously. Victims fear this same power can be used to take actions of reprisal against them or to pay or persuade others to do so. There is also fear of spiritual reprisal. Some religious leaders use the Bible to justify their actions. Throughout this book, there are accounts of ministers who have prodded their victims into sex by using the Bible or promises of spiritual salvation. Trusting or fearing their religious leaders, these victims succumbed to the leader's demands.

ATTENTION

Many mega-church leaders have had adulterous affairs that have become public, while others remain private. Those that remain private include consensual affairs. Unlike children or those molested against their will, the women or men who these leaders cheat with in extramarital affairs make conscious adult decisions to have these affairs, with most knowing the true identity of the church leader. Some are members of the church congregation or on the church staff, while others are from outside of the church. The reasons they engage in these affairs with ministers are numerous. Some do it for the attention. They find pleasure that someone so powerful would be romantically interested in them. Some do it for a sense of conquest, relishing the fact that they could attract such a person and turn them from their faith and family. Others do so thinking they will be able to pull the minister from his current spouse and marry them in turn.

There are also those who do so for attention during times of vulnerability. Because of some issue a person has, he or she may engage in sex with a minister out of a need to deal with that issue. The minister's returned attention becomes a trigger. Ministers serve dual roles as religious leaders and spiritual counselors. Often their members seek advice for marital, financial, and other personal issues. Some mega-church leaders have used these times of vulnerability to coax those seeking counseling into sex. In 2010, Steve C. Robbins, one of nearly 30 associate pastors at the 8,000-member Vineyard Church in Columbus, Ohio, had an almost three-month affair with a church member who originally sought his counseling for sexual addiction. The woman, her husband, and five children, sued 61-year-old Robbins, the church, and Texas-based Vineyard USA (the national office) for failing to stop the relationship. The suit alleged sexual abuse because of Robbins's position of power and because he knew that as a child, the woman had been sexually abused by three men in positions of power. Robbins pressed the woman for sexual details during their counseling sessions, knowing this would sexually excite her and cause a relapse with him. The affair did not end until she sought counseling at an out-of-state treatment facility. Robbins was fired from the church when the incident was made public.

In other cases, ministers may abuse the opportunity of a church member seeking their spiritual attention. Bishop Rick Hawkins founded the massive San Antonio, Texas–based Family Praise Center, a charter school named after him, and an accredited bible college that trains evangelicals. In 2007, he was accused of sexually harassing church members and having adulterous affairs. Several women alleged that he took advantage of them when they came to him for spiritual counseling by soliciting them for phone sex. In addition, he came under investigation for using thousands of dollars in church funds to silence his victims. The church lost hundreds of members. The situation soon became worse and even more controversial. Randy and Paula White founded Without Walls International Church in Tampa, Florida. The church had over 22,000 members until 2008. That year, the Whites announced they were divorcing. Paula White was marrying Hawkins.

Robbins and Hawkins are examples of ministers succumbing to sexual and other urges as a result of counseling sessions. This occurs because most ministers are not trained counselors. Psychologists and psychiatrists have years of educational and professional training centered on helping others while maintaining strict boundaries within the doctor-patient relationship. Because of their training in theology and years of studying religious texts, some ministers believe they are able to provide counseling to anyone seeking it. For those seeking religious counseling, the minster is qualified to provide assistance. However, this is not the case in matters where the person seeking help has a deep-rooted psychological disorder that truly requires assistance from a trained professional. This situation is analogous to those who proclaim to be marriage experts because they have been married to the same person for many years. While they are able to speak on their personal experiences and how they dealt with certain issues, they cannot claim to be experts in all matters of marriage. This is in no way saying ministers should not attempt to assist their members in all manners in which they can. However, ministers must recognize and act upon their deficiencies in areas outside of their expertise. This is often difficult because many (if not most) ministers have a "messiah complex" in which they believe they can use religious teachings to assist anyone in any matter. While these teachings may apply to the situation at hand, there may be other underlying problems the counselee has that must be addressed before they can be addressed by religious advice. Ministers should ensure they have a cadre of experts to consult and refer members to in these situations.

Some people engage in sexual relations with mega-church leaders for money and other gifts. They then remain quiet about their affair because of the financial gains. Ministers in such cases find themselves in similar situations to others with wealth, including actors, politicians, and business leaders. Wealthy men (in slang terms, "sugar daddies," that is, older men who pay for the companionship of a younger person), for example, will not only provide finances in exchange for companionship but also to keep their sexual companion from revealing their affair. In addition to money, their companions are often taken to exclusive hotels and restaurants, treated to lavish trips, and bought expensive jewelry, clothes, and cars. They are also given special attention, making them feel loved and important. There are many downsides to this type of relationship. First, the person paying for companionship may feel ownership of the other. This includes demanding they be available whenever requested, questioning their whereabouts, not allowing them to spend time with friends and family, and withholding support when they are upset. Second, the person being "kept" may find it difficult to ever become involved in a normal relationship. They may develop self-esteem issues resulting from being controlled, or they may gain a reputation as a person who gets involved with others only for money. Third, the person being kept may acquire emotional feelings for the minister. However, these affections will not be returned. In fact, they may cause the minister to leave the situation out of fear the attraction will cause the other person to publicly reveal the relationship. Fourth, the person being kept will begin to request more financial rewards to replace the emotional emptiness of the relationship. Since the relationship is based, in essence, on money in exchange for sex, he or she will eventually ask for more money or more expensive gifts to fill the void of knowing he or she will never have a normal relationship with the minister. When demands become too excessive, the minister will leave. Finally, these types of arrangements are always temporary. Eventually, the minister will either come to his senses and end the affair (unlikely) or find someone new (more likely). The person being kept is then left with nothing. Sometimes he or she is no longer able to afford an apartment, has a car repossessed, and is not even able to turn to the friends or family who probably scorned the relationship from the beginning.

CHILD SEX ABUSE

Child molestation and sexual assault are the darkest side of sexual misconduct. In these cases, the victims are in shock, fear for their safety, and often do not understand what has prompted the unwanted attack. In the midst of these feelings is a lack of knowing exactly how to react. Minors are often fearful of telling their parents or authorities. A large part of this fear comes from threats made by the perpetrator if the child reveals what has happened. Collaterally, there is the fear of somehow being blamed for what happened. This is why most incidents of child molestation do not surface until the victim reaches adulthood (if they are even revealed then).

According to the National Child Traumatic Stress Network, some children who have been sexually abused may take weeks, months, or even years to fully reveal what was done to them.[5] Many children never tell anyone about the abuse. For those who do reveal incidents, the following generally holds true:

- Girls are more likely to disclose than boys.
- School-age children tend to tell a caregiver.
- Adolescents are more likely to tell friends.
- Very young children tend to accidentally reveal abuse because they do not have as much understanding of what occurred or the words to explain it.

Children are often reluctant to reveal they have been sexually abused for several reasons. These include:

- Fear that the abuser may hurt them or members of their family
- Fear that they will not be believed or will be blamed and get in trouble
- Worry that their parents will be upset or angry
- Fear that disclosing will disrupt the family, especially if the perpetrator is a family member or friend
- Fear that if they tell, they will be taken away and separated from their family
- Not understanding what has happened to them is wrong, especially in cases involving younger children

Studies show that youth today are reporting incidents of sexual abuse more so than in the past. In a recent study published in *Pediatrics and Adolescent Medicine* on the results of a survey of 4,549 children and youth conducted from January 1, 2008 through May 31, 2008, researchers found that 45.7 percent of those studied had at least one of their abuse incidents known to school, police, or medical authorities. In the case of serious victimizations such as sexual assault by an adult, kidnapping, and gang assaults, authorities were aware of 70.1 percent or more of the incidents. In general, school officials were more aware of victimizations than were police or medical authorities. This level of awareness was higher than found in studies conducted in 1992. In this 2008 study, "The victimizations most likely to be known were typically of a more serious nature, such as sexual abuse by a known or nonspecified adult (69.0% and 76.1%), kidnapping (73.5%), and gang or group assault (70.1%). However, even emotional bullying (51.5%), neglect (47.8 %), and theft (46.8%) were often known to authorities. The types of episodes least likely to be known were peer and sibling assault (16.9%), dating violence (15.2%), sexual exposure/being flashed (16.6%), completed and attempted rape (14.0%), and statutory rape (3.4%)." However, a troubling finding is that boys are less likely to report incidents. The study also found that "boys are still disproportionately less likely to report, for some of the reasons showcased in this trial: the fear that others will not believe they are really victims, and the fear that they will be stigmatized as wimpy and/or homosexual."[6]

The implications of sexual abuse on children are serious. The impact on their physical and mental well-being can be devastating and last for years. Side effects may include withdrawal, depression, thoughts of suicide, and the children themselves becomes sexual abusers later in life. As Wickham and West discuss in *Therapeutic Work with Sexually Abused Children*, "Child victims of sexuality, beyond their emotional and physical developmental levels, are violated in every sense of the word: physically, psychologically, emotionally, and spiritually."[7] They outline the following problems that may result:

- *Traumatic sexualization:* Conventional sexual behavior is skewed. The child may develop atypical sexual behaviors as a young person and adult.
- *Stigmatization:* The abused child may feel bad, blaming himself or herself for bringing trouble upon the family and maintaining the secrecy enjoined by the perpetrator. The child's self-esteem may be jeopardized, and some children subsequently turn to self-harm, substance abuse, or even suicide. The child may dissociate from the abusive situation.
- *Betrayal:* The child's trust in adults may have been violated, and suspicion of other people and their intentions may intrude their ability to trust.
- *Powerlessness:* Powerlessness can promote victimization, depression, or suicidal behavior. The experience of powerlessness may also lead to the internalization of a victim-persecutor internal working model for relationships, which sows the seeds for the child later becoming a perpetrator when placed in a position where an opportunity to exert power over a vulnerable person arises.

The following statistics outline the damage to the victims of sexual assault according to the Rape, Abuse and Incest National Network:[8]

- 3 times more likely to suffer from depression
- 6 times more likely to suffer from post-traumatic stress disorder
- 13 times more likely to abuse alcohol
- 26 times more likely to abuse drugs
- 4 times more likely to contemplate suicide

Another sad part of children being molested is that they may actually become dependent on their abuser. The minister may make them feel special, offer them escape from an unhappy home environment, and give them elaborate gifts. When the abuse is made public, it can traumatize the victim. Acts or thoughts of suicide are perhaps the most serious outcome of child sexual abuse. A 2004 study published in *Child Abuse & Neglect* analyzed the results of sexual abuse in adolescents. The major findings of the study were that

> sexually abused adolescents were much more likely to report having had thoughts about killing themselves (73% abused, 25% non-abused); to have made plans (to commit suicide) (55% abused, 12% non-abused); to have made threats (45% abused, 9% non-abused); to have deliberately hurt themselves (54% abused, 17% non-abused); and to claim attempt(s) to kill themselves (24% abused, 5% non-abused). In addition, frequency and severity of suicidal behavior appear to be greater amongst sexually abused adolescents. When asked how often they hurt themselves deliberately, 30 percent of abused versus 5 percent of non-abused claimed five or more injuries. Regarding attempts, 32 percent of abused versus 2 percent non-abused had tried to kill themselves five or more times. Further, 36 percent of abused versus 8 percent of non-abused were admitted to hospital, suggesting a medically serious attempt. Gender specific analyses reveal that 55 percent of sexually abused boys versus 3.5 percent of non-abused boys reported attempted suicide, and 29 percent of sexually abused girls versus 6 percent of non-abused girls reported attempted suicide.[9]

The families of sexual abuse victims also suffer. The revelation that their child has been sexually abused by their minister can be devastating. In some cases, it is worse than their child being abused by a family member. There is the betrayal of trust, the revelation of lies that were told by the minister to get near their child and continue a secret relationship, and the pain they feel from the pain their child has experienced. There will be blame placed on the minister and the church, blame on themselves for not noticing the warning signs of sexual abuse, and some blame on the child for not saying anything. Parents may also place misplaced blame on their child for somehow being responsible, but only because of their initial level of anger and guilt.

The decision to take legal action against the minister or report the behavior to the church is part of a difficult process related to weighing alternatives. The family thinks about the costs involved—including losing their privacy and being seen as bad parents—and the shame that comes with being scrutinized by the church, the community, and the media. They must compare these costs to the possible benefits of bringing closure to the abuse inflicted on their family, ensuring the minister is punished for his crime, and preventing other victims and their families from going through the same type of incidents once the minister is punished. A conflicting point is considering how likely it is that the minister will actually be punished.

If they do decide to take legal action, a family faces long legal battles against the minister, which can be both stressful and expensive. Throughout the process, there is the fear of retaliation by the minister and the church. There are so many questions about how to cope with this while trying to live their daily lives. Should they allow their child to go to school? Should they go to work? Should they obtain a restraining order against the minister? Is it safe to attend church? How will they be able to afford court costs? One of the darkest parts of this process is the constant denials of guilt by the minister and the support he seems to be receiving from members of the church. This intensifies the feeling of being betrayed and the anger of their child being portrayed as a liar after they have already gone through so much.

Regardless of their immediate decision about legal action, the child needs both psychological and medical examinations. He or she has to be screened for visible injuries, bodily trauma, and sexually transmitted diseases. Counseling is needed for both the child and the parents for depression, anxiety, and feelings of guilt. Parents have to provide the child with a safe and supportive environment. They must reassure the child that he or she has done nothing wrong, listen, respond to concerns and fears, and closely monitor any changes in behavior. It is imperative parents reassure the child that they believe him or her and that the perpetrator is the only one to blame for what has happened.

Unfortunately, there will be conflicts with church members. It is inevitable because a mega-church has so many members. Neither the parents nor the child can stay isolated forever, and they will eventually face other church members at work, school, or while shopping. They will also face those from outside the church who are aware of the incident through gossip or the media. Some of these people will be supportive, but some may be confrontational. Just as victims often face being blamed for abuse happening to them, families also face this accusation. There are questions of how they allowed their child to be put in a predicament without parental supervision where sexual abuse could happen. Everyone will have the same questions: How did this happen? Didn't you notice anything? What are you going to do? The answer to this last question should be: "What's in the best interest of our child and our family."

Some victims of sexual molestation or assault by church leaders also face the anger of church members. They may be stigmatized in the church and in their communities by members who blame them for what happened. Even if members blame the leader, the victims are seen as being physically and socially tainted. For victims, leading a normal life after incidents are revealed is often difficult or impossible. Some move from their communities. However, mega-church scandals gain national and sometimes international attention. Victims therefore find it difficult to move to areas where they are not known; and if they do move, they constantly they will be identified.

The legal process itself can be daunting and worse than the revelation of the abuse. The child and family will be questioned about every detail of the abuse by law enforcement officials, social service workers, and during the trial. The child will have to recount every intimate detail of the abuse over and over. Regardless of the outcome of the case, there are likely to be both positive and negative consequences. If the perpetrator is convicted, there is relief but also sadness and some level of remorse. This is due to a level of blame the victim has about somehow causing the incident, as well as from confusion about feelings about the perpetrator. If there is a plea deal or the minister is not convicted, there is anger and intense feelings of betrayal. Out-of-court settlements may provide financial gains, but the pain and anger remain. There is also never a feeling of closure.

When the case finally ends legally, there are still issues to deal with. Children may need counseling far into the future. They will often find it difficult to trust adults, especially teachers, coaches, and other ministers. The family has to deal with the loss of their church as well as the support of some of their friends and family members. Leaving their church leaves a void because they are unable to worship and meet their own religious needs. They may feel stigmatized by the incident for years. Even going to another church may not be an immediate option if the news about what they are going through has spread throughout their community. Parents must realize the healing process may be a long and tedious journey, but their child will overcome the pain as long as they remain supportive.

Parents, children, adult victims, and the church must realize the consequences if they do not take action against the perpetrator. Fear is the reason many do not. The fear of reporting incidents in cases of rape, molestation, or even adultery leads the culprit to continue engaging in acts with the same and/or different people. This is evidenced by the many examples given throughout this book where ministers have continued to violate victims until a victim goes public or reports the incidents to authorities. In some cases, a minister has multiple victims. The lack of actions to immediately stop the sexual offender by the first or first few victims contributes to culprits' habitual behavior. This is also the case when the relationship is consensual. There is still extensive damage to the church and the minister as his behavior continues.

PROSTITUTION AND MISTRESSES

Prostitutes are recurring sexual partners in cases of sexual scandals by mega-church leaders. These individuals engage in sex for money with no or little concern for the private or public lives of their clients. In cases of church leaders, few prostitutes seem to have any concern that their client is the leader of church. There are exceptions, such as Mike Jones, who admitted that former pastor Ted Haggard had been a regular client of his for three years up until 2006. Haggard used an alias with Jones, and Jones did not realize Haggard was a church leader until he saw him on television. Once he realized it, he came forward and publicly disclosed the sexual incidents. Other prostitutes, however, remain anonymous forever, or at least until the event is disclosed by someone else. Of course, it is the mega-church leader who solicits for their services. Still, prostitutes provide an available—although illegal—avenue for church leaders and others to engage in sex with some degree of anonymity.

Televangelist Jimmy Swaggart is perhaps one of the best known mega-church leaders whose downfall resulted from frequenting prostitutes. In 1986, he began public attacks against televangelists Marvin Gorman and Jim Bakker for their infidelities. In retaliation, Gorman hired a private investigator who uncovered Swaggart's affair with a prostitute. On February 21, 1998, Swaggart made a memorable and tearful apology on his television program, stating,

And to the hundreds of millions that I have stood before in over a hundred countries of the world, and I've looked into the cameras and so many of you with a heart of loneliness, needing help, have reached out to the minister of the gospel as a beacon of light. You that are nameless—most I will never be able to see except by faith. I have sinned against you. I beg you to forgive me. And most of all, to my Lord and my Savior, my Redeemer, the One whom I have served and I love and I worship. I bow at His feet, who has saved me and washed me and cleansed me. I have sinned against You, my Lord. And I would ask that Your precious blood would wash and cleanse every stain, until it is in the seas of God's forgetfulness, never to be remembered against me anymore.[10]

Swaggart was removed from his church and lost his ministerial license. However, his misconduct did not stop there. In 1991, he was stopped by a California police officer for driving on the wrong side of the road. During this stop, Swaggart was found with a prostitute in his car who admitted Swaggart had solicited her for sex.

In April 2010, Christian leader George Alan Rekers, who was 61 at the time, was photographed returning to Miami International Airport from a two-week European vacation with a 20-year-old gay male prostitute. The prostitute advertised his services as being a "rent boy." Rekers was an activist against homosexuality and cofounder of the Family Research Council, a Christian lobbying organization that supports socially conservative policies including opposing any laws that support homosexuality. He was also formerly an officer of and scientific advisor for the National Association for Research and Therapy of Homosexuality. The organization offered therapy to "cure" homosexuals into becoming heterosexuals. Rekers was even used as an expert witness against gay couples seeking to adopt.

Mega-church leaders frequent prostitutes for many of the same reasons as others do. Prostitutes offer emotionally detached sex and are willing to act out their clients' fantasies for the right price. Their services are provided without emotion, and both parties are aware of what they are giving and receiving within their paid time together. Prostitutes are sexual actors who will say and do anything to make their clients feel good about the experience and good about themselves. Clients frequent them as a means of escape from their marriages, to relieve the stress of work and self-esteem issues, and because they want anonymous sex with someone willing to engage in whatever sexual act they want. In some cases, a prostitute performs sexual acts a client's spouse will not do or that the client is too embarrassed to ask his spouse to do. Sometimes, these are acts the client does not want his spouse to do out of respect and the desire to have a wholesome spouse at home. This is especially true of ministers. Prostitutes also allow people to have encounters in a relatively safe environment where their affairs will not be made public. However, many clients feel deep shame and regret after their encounters. These feelings are accompanied by feelings of loneliness and guilt.

For church leaders, this guilt is often threefold. There is the guilt of betraying their spouses, their congregations, and also their faith. First, they are cheating on their spouse no matter how they may try to justify it otherwise. Some men feel they are not cheating because they have no emotional connection to the prostitute. However, if the spouse finds out the person their husband cheated with was a prostitute, reconciliation is not likely. This is especially true if the situation is made public. Second, their actions are morally wrong in the context of both societal norms and per the edicts of the church. It violates such edicts as adultery, self-control, and contributing to the further downfall of someone who already is suffering from a lack of moral fortitude. Last, soliciting a prostitute is illegal is almost every state (except for a small number of localities in Nevada). Those prosecuted face punishments ranging from fines to jail time.

Any feelings of remorse the minister does feel are detached when sexual urges return and overcome any feelings of trepidation in obtaining hired services again. This results in a cycle of using prostitutes and feeling shame. The most abhorrent are those who feel no guilt; rather, they justify their actions due to the stress of their jobs and the need for sexual gratification regardless of their offenses and the possible consequences of their actions.

Although mistresses are not committing illegal acts, some share the same motive as prostitutes in that they too provide companionship and sex based upon the financial benefits they receive. The primary difference is that a mistress may have sex with only the one person providing them benefits versus anyone who pays. Some go so far as being "kept." Their housing and all of their financial support is provided by the person they are having an affair with. The attractiveness of their arrangement is that they receive benefits without any full-time relationship obligations or commitment. Some are not seeking marriage and are actually happy the person taking care of them is married. This gives them the freedom to engage in other activities they enjoy with friends and family. However, there is also a great deal of stress in being a mistress. A mistress has to deal with the issue of a partner who is not fully committed to a relationship having a degree of control over the mistress' life because of financial support being provided. There are also broken promises because the man the mistress is involved with cannot sneak away from his spouse or obligations to family and work. There is also the realization that the man will never really leave his family for his mistress. At some point, the man will leave his mistress.

Mistresses provide more than just sex, and sex is not the only need a man's wife may not be fulfilling that led him to seek an affair. They provide an escape from a person's everyday life. They are an escape from the everyday realities of family and work responsibilities, they provide a feeling of reclaiming or rekindling one's youth, and they provide a feeling of being masculine that is not satisfied by the wife. They may also provide a social relationship that the wife no longer does or never did in the same way. The man may feel his mistress is someone he can really "open up to" and that she truly understands his perceptions on different issues and life in general. At the same time, she is not judgmental or dismissive of his feelings. However, all of these benefits are from the point of view of the man. The mistress, on the other hand, is in essence a victim who satisfies the physical and mental needs of the man in exchange for money. All of her listening and being attentive to his physical needs could be just an act to ensure her revenue stream does not go away. At the same time, she may tolerate his behavior because she knows he is not a full-time partner and is willing to commit a few hours a day or week to giving him attention.

Some mistresses desire a long-term commitment. However, most men make it clear to their mistresses that their relationship is based only on sex and that they will never leave their wives. The majority, however, do not make this clear. They paint their wives as villains and themselves as hopeless victims in a sterile marriage. They may speak of wanting to leave their wife but also of the many reasons they cannot. These include not being able to afford alimony or child support, the necessity to stay married for the sake of his children, and the need to maintain the portrait of a happy marriage because of church duties and their position in the community. However, married men in general seldom leave for their wives for their mistresses. Most are not looking for another long-term commitment; rather, they are seeking excitement and a distraction from their current life. They most likely still have feelings for their wife. They are also not willing to face a divorce or leave their children for a person they know is willing to having an affair with a married man.

Even when a man considers a committed relationship with his mistress, he often does not for fear of the consequences. Divorcing his wife in the midst of a situation of infidelity could lead to large alimony and child support payments. He could also lose custody of his children. He is not willing to trade a current unhappy marriage for what could turn into another unhappy long-term commitment. There is also the concern of how family, friends, neighbors, and coworkers will respond. This is in addition to being concerned about how his wife's family and friends will respond. Marriages that result from affairs are not generally viewed as socially acceptable.

For ministers, being a church leader is the primary reason they will never leave their wife for a mistress. They do not want to deal with the scandal, especially when the woman they left her for was his former mistress. Even if they did, it would be unlikely the church would be willing to accept such a woman as the first lady in the church. There will be the eventual public disclosure of how the two met, whether through formal investigation by the church or the rumor mill. This disclosure will involve publicly revealing the church leader committed adultery. Other concerns are similar to those normal couples have to deal with. Who will get custody of the children? How much alimony will have to be paid (especially with the minister being so wealthy)? Who will get possession of the home as well as other property and assets? How will the minister and the wife be able to maintain their current lifestyle if their income from the church ends?

Another issue is the psychological effects of dealing with a divorce. Married couples become accustomed to the routines of their married life. This comfort level becomes greater the longer the two are married. The decision to divorce may take years, and outside influences such as discovering a spouse is having an affair may be required to finally go through with it. As Clarke-Stewart and Brentano discuss in *Divorce: Causes and Consequences*,

From a social exchange perspective, the divorce decision involves a cost-benefit analysis of the pros and cons of leaving the marriage. The unhappy spouse considers the barriers to divorce—for example, religious restrictions, obligations to children, the financial costs and consequences of divorce, and social pressers to stay married. These barriers are weighed against the alternative attractions outside the marriage—for example, a more peaceful life, a better partner, or greater individual freedom. If the alternative attractions outweigh the perceived benefits of the marriage and the costs of divorce, the spouse may decide to end the marriage. The extent to which this analysis is a conscious and rational process differs for different individuals. In addition, for some people, the process is fairly quick; for others it takes years or even decades. It is not uncommon for significant problems to exist in a marriage long before a divorce. Often, individuals vacillate in their decision making for years, chalking up one more violation, another broken promise, until, with the discovery of infidelity or a final violent episode, they arrive at a clear decision.[11]

Chapter 4

The Silence of the Church: Is It Supporting the Minister in His Sexual Misdeeds?

The structures of U.S. mega-churches are odd in the context of U.S. history and culture. The United States is a nation founded on the principle of a government with checks and balances to prevent corruption under the power of a single person or group of people. Americans apply that same principle to basically every aspect of life. Large corporations are managed by boards of directors, large universities are run by boards of regents, and large communities have homeowner's associations. Even though all of these entities have a single person overseeing daily management (a chief executive officer [CEO], chairman, principal, or president), there is some board or group that has ultimate authority and oversight. However, mega-church congregations basically allow their leader to exert majority control over the church by nature of their sometimes unwavering faith in the leader's message and direction. Even when these churches reach the point of having tens of thousands of members, satellite sites around the country, and influence around the globe, the minister still maintains primary control of the church and the running of its business.

In *Exploring the Megachurch Phenomena: Their Characteristics and Cultural Context*, Scott Thumma discussed and provided examples of how the organization of mega-churches allows for an authoritative organization with the leader having control of all facets of the church can lead to an abuse of power and sexual indiscretions. He stated that

> the organizational structures in place (a successful charismatic leader, with centralized power, few checks and balances, and perhaps inadequate management and leadership training) clearly allow for this possibility. The claims of abuse by leadership and a lack of accountability, especially for nondenominational mega-churches, are frequent charges heard from former members and external critics. Jack Hyles, minister of the very large First Baptist Church of Hammond, Indiana, his son, and several staff members have all been accused many times in recent years of sexual and authority abuses. Hyles has denied the allegations; however, they continue to plague his ministry. Chapel Hill Harvester Church in Atlanta has also had numerous charges of sexual and authority abuse made against its leadership.[1]

As this discussion from Thumma details, the power of the church in the hands of a single person creates a situation of two dual primary concerns. First is the possibility for acts of financial and sexual misconduct due to the lack of accountability and oversight. As the head of their churches, mega-church leaders have the ability to block any attempts by church members to establish an oversight process. Second is the survival of the church if a leader is ousted, retires, or dies. The ability to have a succession that maintains or expands the church's influence is difficult. Unfortunately, this is the situation in almost all mega-churches.

Mega-churches are autonomous because in most cases their minister started the church and grew it into a massive organization or was appointed minister after the church was established but led in its growth. They are also autonomous in their operations because they are nondenominational, that is, not affiliated with an organized religious body. Because of mega churches' tax-exempt status, the only outside oversight is financial monitoring by the government. But this is difficult because churches self-report their revenues and expenses. The Internal Revenue Service (IRS) does, however, have oversight of churches to ensure they truly are nonprofit, and the organization can audit suspected churches and their leaders who have been accused of misusing church funds for personal use if those funds are not fully reimbursed. The following are the criteria required by the IRS for churches to obtain and maintain their tax-exempt status:[2]

- The organization must be organized and operated exclusively for religious, educational, scientific, or other charitable purposes.
- Net earnings may not inure to the benefit of any private individual or shareholder.

- No substantial part of its activity may be attempting to influence legislation.
- The organization may not intervene in political campaigns.
- The organization's purposes and activities may not be illegal or violate fundamental public policy.

Investigations are conducted when churches are suspected of wrongdoing, but there must be reasonable and reliable information leading to the investigation. For example, the IRS, Secret Service, and DeKalb County, Georgia, police began an investigation of Eddie Long's New Birth Missionary Baptist Church in 2011 after former church members accused the church of conspiracy to defraud them of their retirement savings through "wealth building" seminars. The laptops of church employees were seized, and the former church members sued the church.[3]

Mega-church leaders also have such power and authority because the church becomes more business-like as it grows. Staff members and assistant ministers begin adopting a more work-like attitude toward their jobs rather than drive based on a religious mission. With this attitude comes the desire to protect their jobs and incomes even when things in the church are not going as they are supposed to. Rather than a single focus on the church's mission, they become focused on administrative functions related to running offices, financial management, property management, and human resource management. The minister assumes a CEO-like position, overseeing church operations. This includes not only finances and personnel management, but also oversight of all the programs the church establishes to support its members. This includes day care, athletics, satellite site operations, and even parking. All of this secularizes the church because more detail is paid to managing activities than delivering a message. Mega-churches do have assistant ministers and staff leads who oversee the various operations of the church and advise the minister. In comparison to private business, they act as a quasi-board of directors. Unlike in businesses, however, they are not chosen impartially. They are either chosen or approved by the minister because of their personal relationship to him, service to the church, or perceived ability. However, the minister ensures each is someone he can personally trust and to some degree control.

With secularism comes the probability of cynicism and corruption. This impacts the church congregation. The members of small churches feel directly and intimately involved in their churches. In mega-churches, many or most may feel detached from church operations. For example, they have to adhere to bureaucratic procedures to even talk personally with their minister, whereas most had constant communication with the church leader when the church was small. After services, some mega-churches have ushers who act more like bodyguards in screening members who want to even shake the minister's hand. The secularism of church staff and leaders coupled with the detachment of church members contribute a propensity for wrongdoing to go unnoticed, be ignored, or be allowed to continue.

Any acts of wrongdoing by church leaders not only reflect their own failings, but also reflect negatively on their churches. This is especially the case with sex abuse or sexual misconduct. As Matthews points out in *Sexual Abuse of Power in the Black Church: Sexual Misconduct in the African American Churches*,

> Ethically speaking, any behavior in which a person is used as an object is abusive. In this case it involves using a person for one's own sexual gratification despite the negative effects involved in that behavior. The pastor who engages in sexual misconduct with his members is engaging in activity in which his power as a spiritual leader is misused for reasons that are ultimately harmful to him, his victim, his church, and his family. The entire system of church and family are harmed by his abusive actions. Because the pastor is the primary role model and leader of the congregation he sets the terms by example for ethical and unethical behavior in the church. His actions will have a profound effect on the spiritual and psychological well-being of his church and community.[4]

One of the reasons church ministers, pastors, and priests are able to engage in acts of sexual misconduct is because their congregations and church leaders remain silent even when they know these acts are taking place. Even in the cases of ministers molesting children and having sex with adolescents, some churches take no action to sanction or remove their church leader, report suspicions, or given evidence to authorities. The Roman Catholic Church has been accused of doing this for centuries. However, this also occurs in mega-churches. For example, Greater St. Stephen Baptist Church in New Orleans had a membership that grew from 647 to 20,000 in the 1980s. In the late 1990s, church members and leaders were aware that their minister of music, Philip Britton, was having sex with a 16-year-old male church member. Even the church leader, Paul Morton, was aware. However, no one took action to help the young man, who later made it public Britton had exposed him to HIV. The church membership included some of the most powerful public figures in the city, including a U.S. congressman. After the child's mother found out what was happening, she attempted to contact the church for help. However, no one would even return her phone calls. The young man and his mother reported to police in October 1999 that Britton had engaged in anal and oral sex with the boy over 100 times during a one-year period that began in July 1998. Another church employee was accused of letting Britton use his apartment to have sex with the boy. When Britton was finally brought to trial, he was given only a $500 fine and six months of inactive probation.[5]

Not reporting and not removing a minister leads to even greater harm to victims. It may cause them mental harm that lasts for years or even the rest of their life. As Horst points out in *Questions and Answers about Clergy Misconduct*, "Many offending clergy claim that they are the true victims when reports of their inappropriate behavior become public. The reality is, even when claims are substantiated, offending clergy often continue in ministry. Victims, more often than not, lose their spiritual home and perhaps even their spiritual life. Many struggle for years with psychological issues created or exacerbated by the victimization: shame, depression, anxiety disorders, addictions. When the 'affair' is over, the one with less power will suffer more."[6]

Churches are protective of their internal affairs. This crosses all denominations, and occurs in both organized religions and single churches. Finances, issues with members, personnel and staff matters, and especially the private lives of their leaders are kept confidential by the church leadership. In *Understanding Clergy Misconduct in Religious Systems: Scapegoating, Family Secrets, and the Abuse of Power*, Benyei aptly describes this behavior as being a Pandora's box of secrets. She states, "Like Pandora's box, congregations are often containers of all sorts of secrets. In the case of clergy misconduct, they will also be containers of not only abuse, but distrust, anger, fear betrayal, paralysis, and a legion of other diseases. Unlike, Pandora, however, congregants are for the most part not curious about the contents and wish the lid to remain tightly closed. In fact, they punish anyone who would reveal the contents for fear that the family of faith will be harmed. They enforce a 'zone of silence' around undiscussable matters, creating odd gaps in communication and record keeping."[7]

One of the primary reasons churches remain quiet when they know their leaders are engaging in acts of sexual misconduct is to protect their churches' image. Members of churches that have grown from a few hundred to thousands of members have pride in their accomplishments and the church's mission to members and the community. This pride, however, is sometimes uncompromisable even when the well-being of a few is at stake. They feel that accusations against their minister or others in high positions within the church will cause members to leave, public support to wane, and donations to decrease or cease. They also feel they will be publicly stigmatized as members of a church where such actions by leaders have taken place. Even those that are outraged do not want to be labeled whistleblowers. There is too much fear of retaliation by the minister and other members of the church.

When cases of sexual misconduct are made public internal or external to the church, the leaders directly under the minister (such as assistant ministers or deacons) may conduct their own review. In most cases, this is done so that it appears they are taking serious actions in order to calm concerns of inactiveness by the church. They will therefore internally investigate accusations of sexual misconduct but keep their findings private. They do so under the guise of the issue being a religious matter that cannot and should not be handled by the secular world. What is troubling is that they do not reveal the findings of their investigations to the victims, the victims' families, or law enforcement officials. The case of Bob Moorehead provides an example. Moorehead served as the senior pastor of the 6,500-member, $37.5 million Overlake Christian Church in Redmond, Washington, beginning in 1970. Even when he was accused of sexual misconduct by 17 victims and had been arrested for indecent exposure in a public restroom, the church dismissed all allegations against him based upon the results of what they called the "biblical process" for handling accusations against a church leader. Moorehead resigned only because the public revelation of the case damaged his credibility in the community. The church hired a private investigator to interview the accusers. However, church leaders interpreted the Bible to require a witness in addition to the accuser to collaborate the accusations before they would act. In cases of sexual misconduct or abuse, rarely is there ever a witness. In a statement to the church, church leadership said, "This is not like a secular case, where conviction can be based on a preponderance of evidence, or evidence that's beyond a reasonable doubt. Ours is a biblical investigation."[8] Church leadership also communicated to their members that their church was under an orchestrated attack by the media and the accusers to persecute the church.

This case exemplifies the stances many mega-churches take when their leaders are accused of sexual misconduct, whether the accusations are alleged or proven to be true. They first denounce any outside investigations by law enforcement officials and then rely on their own. In some cases, their internal investigations are real efforts to find out the truth; in others, they are mere pretenses to stave off criticisms. Regardless, their investigations are not impartial and often do even more damage to victims who may feel they are being interrogated rather than interviewed. The church then demonizes victims and public scrutiny to church members to maintain member loyalty and attendance. For those members who may be skeptical, choice information is provided. To show impartial loyalty, initial information is provided by someone other than the minister. This gives the perception that the members of the church must support the minister because other senior church leaders do. Eventually, the church leader addresses the accusations in writing or in a verbal statement, being careful to deny accusations and self-blame. This is done to protect the church and him from criminal charges and potential lawsuits.

Behind the scenes is a team of lawyers on the payroll of the church who may have dealt with similar situations in other churches or in the private sector. They prepare themselves, the minister, and other church leaders for dealing with allegations weeks or even months before the allegations are made public. In some cases, before any public disclosure, they contact victims to first persuade them to remain silent and next to offer out-of-court settlements that they know are below what the victims would receive in court. The ultimate goal is to stop any legal convictions of wrongdoing. These settlements include "gag orders" forbidding the victims from revealing any details of the incident or settlement to anyone under penalty of having to repay the settlement and face charges of breach of contract. The minister is then free to resume his duties and even speak publicly about the false allegations against him. The fact that a settlement has been reached may be made public but communicated as a way to speed the healing process for the church as well as the minister and his family.

The larger the church, the more prone it is to engage in cover-ups. This is primarily because larger churches have the most to lose financially and reputation-wise. Their size also gives them a feeling of superiority along with the ability to control people and situations. Considerable resources are expended in controlling information and people. Those that cannot be controlled are no longer privy to certain information, removed from their position of leadership, and sometimes so ostracized that they leave the church.

Churches also remain quiet to maintain the status quo. This is an excellent example of groupthink. In simple terms, individuals within a group censor their individualism to maintain harmony within the group. This causes them to not weigh the alternatives during decision-making processes but simply go along with the majority opinion. Researchers point to five antecedent conditions that result in groupthink: (1) a high level of group cohesiveness, (2) insulation of the group members from opinions or information from outside the group, (3) an inefficient procedure for gathering and interpreting information, (4) leadership that is both directive and influential, and (5) a high degree of stress and a tendency to avoid challenging the first acceptable alternative suggested by an influential member.[9]

It is easy to see how this situation exists in a mega-church. The church congregation is highly cohesive given they are protective of their church and the influence of its leader. Members receive select information that the church leader and others in positions of authority choose to share. When an act of sexual misconduct occurs, church members are insulated from details of the incident and provided only the select information church leaders choose to release. In most cases, information is purposely distorted to point guilt at the accusers. This process is ineffective in that it can be deceptive and foster confusion in the church. However, sometimes creating this confusion is done intentionally to create a smoke screen. It causes members to focus on a host of issues instead of the primary reason for chaos. The leader of the church and his senior staff are completely directive in all church matters, and their influence lies in their power and influence. The church is thus run by what can be called promotional leadership: the church leader promotes his personal preferences. Last, there is a high degree of stress in these situations given the uncertainty of the future of the minister and the church. When issues of sexual misconduct or embezzlement arise, the majority of the church will follow the direction of the minister or other senior church leader. This is comparable in businesses to "following the company line."

Irving L. Janis documented eight symptoms of groupthink in *Victims of Groupthink* and later in *Groupthink: Psychological Studies of Policy Decisions and Fiascoes.* Again, it easy to see how these symptoms exist in mega-churches:[10]

- *Illusion of invulnerability:* Creates excessive optimism that encourages taking extreme risks. Mega-churches may feel they are invulnerable because they have so many members and so much money, and their minister has so much power due to his personal charisma. They are therefore optimistic they can overcome any crisis that arises. Their optimism lies not only in their secular power, but also in the belief that their religious foundations place them above any secular issues.
- *Collective rationalization:* Members discount warnings and do not reconsider their assumptions. Because mega-churches are so tight-knit in terms of their collective theology tied to a single individual, they may ignore the warning signs of wrongdoing. An accompanying lack of connection to an organized religion and the oversight that comes with this hierarchical structure creates blinders for church members and staff.
- *Belief in inherent morality:* Members believe in the righteousness of their cause and therefore ignore the ethical or moral consequences of their decisions. Most mega-churches operate under a fundamental foundation of religion based upon core values that drive the church's mission and

services. This may cause them to ignore the moral and ethical downfalls of their church leader because he is the foundation of their church.

- *Stereotyped views of out-groups:* Negative views of the "enemy" make effective responses to conflict seem unnecessary. The secular world in general may be deemed the enemy. Attacks on the church's minister are initially deemed slanderous targeted attacks to destroy the minister and the church. The first response is to ignore them. Not until hard evidence or the minister's open confession is presented does the church as a whole concede this position.

- *Direct pressure on dissenters:* Members are under pressure not to express arguments against any of the group's views. Senior members of the staff carefully monitor comments provided by church members and speak or otherwise take action against anyone that makes a statement against the general view of the church.

- *Self-censorship:* Doubts and deviations from the perceived group consensus are not expressed. Individual members seldom, if ever, speak out against the minister, church leaders, or the church's theology. Because they join the church voluntarily, they are free to leave if they disagree with any of these entities. In cases of sexual misconduct, members hold their criticisms until they feel they are amply convinced the allegations are true. They then may decide to leave the church.

- *Illusion of unanimity:* The majority view and judgments are assumed to be unanimous. There is no way members of a mega-church can ever speak to or get to know all of the other members. However, there is a general feeling (perception) or consensus (agreement) that they share the same views on major issues. By fostering an array of services and small groups, mega-churches go to great lengths to make each member feel like he or she is part of the church.

- *Self-appointed "mindguards":* Members protect the group and the leader from information that is problematic or contradictory to the group's cohesiveness, view, and/or decisions. In mega-churches, members do what they can to protect the image of the church and the minister. Some members strive for high positions in the church to protect its image.

Groupthink results in creating a synergistic environment in which each person feels a vital part of the whole. This builds individual commitment and loyalty to an organization. It brings those with shared values and goals closer together. In large companies, it is used to create a corporate culture. The same holds true for mega-churches. They too each have a culture that identifies who they are, what they stand for, and how they meet the needs of their members. This culture goes beyond just being a religious organization. Each has an identifiable ideology that identifies what the church stands for. This is part of the branding or marketing strategy of the church, which is primarily based upon the teachings and ideology of the church's minister.

The groupthink in mega-churches speaks not only to the ability of ministers to instill religious fervor in members, but also to gain their collective loyalty to the minister and the church. Members are pressured by others (peer pressure) and the church authority (leader pressure) to conform to church theology, decision making, and tactics to achieve its mission. Those who do not support the ideas are persuaded to change their dissenting opinions. As part of their marking strategies, mega-churches profess to be open to new ideas, but these ideas must conform to church ideology. For example, churches that do not support abortion will not accept ideas to the contrary.

No one within a mega-church wants to "rock the boat" by being involved in an investigation of the church leader, an action that could cause extreme unrest both within and outside the church. They believe that if they ignore the situation and continue with church business as normal, the situation will just go away and controversy will fade. This is expected of such entities as the Roman Catholic Church, which operates based upon hundreds of years of stalwart tradition. However, mega-churches are established based upon reshaping religious faith and worship in their communities. They engage in activities that attempt to reshape other aspects of society such as holding rallies against abortion and homosexuality, denouncing organizations and individuals who support such causes, and providing direct support to people facing oppression around the world. Yet many remain silent and take no action against sexual misconduct by church leaders. The desire to keep peace within in the church, even a false peace—along with the desire to remain autonomous—outweighs the need to stop leader misbehavior. In *Why Ministers Fall: In Search of the Holy Grail*, Mastrogiovanni describes how churches handle acts of immorality by remaining silent:[11]

Today, immorality in the local church and its leadership has become "fashionably gratuitous." In response, we put mechanisms and methods in place (locally and denominationally), so we don't have to directly touch the situation. Discovering the core of such situations and bringing true biblical healing is like trying to unscramble eggs; many find it overwhelming and impractical. In the end, the effort required to bring healing is tedious and time-consuming. I've witnessed many liken the solution to a move in a Monopoly game: "Go directly to jail and lose a turn. Don't pass Go! Don't collect two hundred dollars!" Because of our reluctance to handle the debris, many times the situation does not turn out favorably; the congregation fools itself into believing they can move forward and those in charge fall back on the rationalization of, "We are simply following procedure." When things get hard some overseers quickly wash their hands of the matter like Pontius Pilate, proclaiming that the offender, or offended, did not want to fully participate in the prescribed process.

Another reason mega-churches do not always take actions against their ministers is general disbelief by church members that their leader could have committed any immoral act. There is also a general feeling that he was subjected to extreme temptation or some conspiracy if he did. The faith that some church members place in their religious leader is sometimes unwavering. They join the church and make an oath to support the church through the most difficult of times. When their church leader is accused of a wrongdoing, especially of a sexual nature, it will take hard evidence or a confession from the leader himself for some to truly belief any accusations. Even with that, many are extremely forgiving. Their faith teaches them forgiveness and patience. This leads them to conclude their leader is "only human" and subject to falling to some temptations. His failing is forgivable, as most religions teach forgiveness by those who themselves wish forgiveness for their own sins.

One does have to ask how far forgiveness goes. The issue with forgiveness is that some mega-church leaders use the faith and forgiveness of their members against them. They use it to take advantage of members sexually and financially, and then ask forgiveness for their wrongdoings only when they are caught. However, they continue their misconduct once that forgiveness has been obtained. As discussed earlier, Jimmy Swaggart begged forgiveness of his membership for having sex with a prostitute. However, he engaged with another prostitute once the first story had blown over.

Darrell Gilyard provides another example. In 2009, he was sentenced to three years in prison after pleading guilty to molesting a teenage girl from his Jacksonville, Florida, church and sending lewd messages to another. He was charged with two counts of lewd conduct involving the sexually explicit text messages and one count of lewd molestation for fondling a teenage girl whose parents brought her to him for counseling. The girls were 14 and 15 at the time. Under the terms of a plea agreement, Gilyard (the former minister of Shiloh Metropolitan Baptist Church in Jacksonville) was required to register as a sex offender in addition to serving an additional three years of sex-offender probation, which limited his contact with children and where he could live and work. Before coming to Shiloh, he was a minister at the Victory Baptist Church in Richardson, Texas, while still in his 20s. He left Victory and came to Shiloh in 1993. According to court records, Victory quietly settled a sexual misconduct allegation against him in 1996. Before being arrested for molesting the girls but also in 2009, Gilyard and Shiloh church settled another lawsuit filed by a woman who said he raped and impregnated her during a 2004 counseling session. The terms of the settlement were confidential. Terms of his probation for child molestation included him not being able to live within 1,000 feet or work at a school or other place where children regularly gather. He could not have any unsupervised contact with children without court permission, had to undergo psychosexual counseling, and was subject to electronic monitoring.

Gilyard was released from prison in December 2011. In January 2012, he became the minister at the Christ Tabernacle Missionary Church in Jacksonville, Florida. Children were not allowed to attend his sermons, and the other conditions of his probation also remained in effect. Once he assumed the ministry, protestors began to stand outside the church, but attendance at the church began to increase once he took over. A deacon for the church explained that they allowed Gilyard to become their minister because both the church and Gilyard were once down and both needed to get back up.[12]

Gilyard is not an extreme case. His is but one of many instances in which a minister commits the same or similar acts of sexual misconduct over and over again once he is forgiven by the church. Like so many other cases, Gilyard's churches arranged out-of-court settlements to protect its image. Church members resent attention from the secular world on the internal affairs of the church. They view this attention as intrusion by the very world the church offers them escape from. Members of the media, law enforcement authorities, and social service workers are all seen as "minions of the devil" whose true motives are to unjustly destroy their leader and their church. Church members feel this intrusion is somehow just as bad as or worse than the actions of their leader and will protect him from this scrutiny by becoming obstinately supportive. They refuse to contribute any information that could support claims of misconduct, become more involved in church activities, and become openly suspicious of any new members or visitors to church events.

Often, church leaders abuse others because they feel they are entitled. In other words, they feel they are justified in their actions due to their service to the church and to their members. Some church members, staff, and other church leaders support the minister because they too feel he is entitled to indiscretions. As McClintock points out in *Sexual Abuse in Congregations: A Resource for Leaders*, "People in power have used their privileged positions to behave as they pleased with people in the parish, and too many bystanders have supported them in their sense of entitlement. One of the manifestations of this entitled feeling can include demands for sexual favors. Entitlement leads to the abuse of power, one form of which is sexual and includes harassment, molestation, and sexual assault. To prevent sexual abuse, an honest appraisal of the power dynamics in the organization is essential. The inappropriate use of power needs to be named and stopped."[13]

Supporting this sense of entitlement may come with huge costs. Members who do not support this stance leave the church. For example, Bernice King, daughter of Dr. Martin Luther King, Jr., was one of the prominent members who left the church of Eddie Long when he was suspected of having sex with male minors.[14] At that time, many in the church still supported Long. While members of the church may feel the minister is entitled, this view is not held by many outside parties connected to the church. This includes outside donors, suppliers, associated churches, and religious associations. The church may find itself completely stigmatized and isolated.

The financial costs of churches remaining silent can be huge. The Roman Catholic Church offers an example of what may result. It paid millions of dollars as a result of sexual abuse cases brought against priests. As Cozzens details in *The Changing Face of the Priesthood: A Reflection on the Priest's Crisis of Soul*, "by the end of the mid 1990s, it was estimated that some six hundred priests had been named in abuse cases and more than half a billion dollars had been paid in jury awards, settlements and legal fees."[15] The cost to the church in the United States is estimated to have reached $3 billion and continued to increase.[16] A great deal of this money was spent on out-of-court settlements given there have been so few arrests of Catholic priests alleged to have sexually abused victims.

Sadly, both organized religions and large individual churches often do not take action against a known pattern of sexual abuse until lawsuits arise. Their financial stability may provide them a false sense of security until costs quickly start to escalate. The Roman Catholic Church is not the only religious entity to have experienced this. In 2012, an Alameda County Superior Court jury in Oakland, California, ordered the Jehovah Witnesses to pay $21 million in punitive damages to a 26-year-old woman for the sexual abuse she experienced as a girl by one of the church's members. These damages were on top of $7 million in compensatory damages she was also awarded. The jury found that the elders who managed the church's congregation in the 1990s and who were under the supervision of Watchtower Bible and Tract Society of New York (the Jehovah's Witnesses' legal entity) knew the church member had recently been convicted of the sexual abuse of another child, but they kept his past record secret from the congregation.[17]

The Mormon Church paid $3 million in just one settlement in 2001 involving a priest molesting young boys for more than a decade in Oregon. Similar settlements were reached in separate cases in other Mormon churches.[18] An article in the *Houston Chronicle* read,

The church that is known for placing a spiritual premium on family values is under increasing attack for an alleged failure to protect its children from pedophiles. Therein lies the irony of a barrage of lawsuits and general complaints alleging that—in an effort to protect its wholesome image—the Church of Jesus Christ of Latter-day Saints, commonly called the Mormon Church, has failed to root out child molesters in its midst. The fast-growing institution, with 10 million members worldwide, is not the only church that has been plagued in recent years by embarrassing cases involving sexual abuse of children. But while Mormon officials maintain that they have eliminated most of the problems that may have once existed, lawsuits and criminal charges linking the church to pedophiles have continued to mount.[19]

According to the Associated Press, the three companies that insure a majority of Protestant churches say they typically receive upward of 260 reports a year of children younger than 18 being sexually abused by members of the clergy, church staff members, volunteers or congregants. Protestants' membership numbers are harder to obtain because the denominations are less centralized than the Roman Catholic Church. Many congregations are independent, making reporting even more difficult. Some of the numbers are from three insurers: the Church Mutual Insurance Company, the GuideOne Insurance Company, and the Brotherhood Mutual Insurance Company. Together, they insure 165,495 churches and worship centers—mostly Protestant congregations—for liability against child sexual abuse and other sexual misconduct. They also insure more than 5,500 religious schools, camps, and other organizations.[20]

Because each mega-church operates as a single entity, the total costs they have collectively or even individually incurred in cases where ministers were accused of sexual misconduct is not known. Like other denominations and individual churches, most cases are settled out of court. Individual cases that have been reported involve lawsuits of sometimes millions of dollars. There are court costs, lawyer fees, out-of-court expenses, and insurance claims that drive the cost of sex cases. On top of this are lost revenues from members who leave the church and outside donators who distance themselves. These costs, along with the negative publicity of a sex scandal, can cause a mega-church to close.

As discussed in other chapters, most cases of sex abuse go unreported. When cases are known within the church, the perpetrator may be allowed to resign rather than be fired. This not only happens in churches, but also in businesses, school systems, and government agencies. This allows the victims to feel that actions have been taken, while giving the organization a legal loophole if lawsuits arise later. However, the perpetrators' personnel records are not annotated to reflect wrongdoing, they are not formally charged with any crime, and they are free to get a job wherever they wish. In some cases, their old organization will even give them glowing references for future jobs. This allows the perpetrator to be hired by other organizations and commit the same types of abuse again. Those released from one church will take a job in another and then another until their abuses are made public.

DOES THE WIFE KNOW?

In sex scandals involving mega-church leaders, there is always the question of whether the spouse had any knowledge of what was occurring. With crimes such as embezzlement, the answer to this question more obvious. Spouses are aware if the houses, cars, travel costs, and other purchases made by their spouses are outside of their means. The salaries of church leaders are publicly revealed. However, given many factors, in the case of sexual misconduct, the signs are much more difficult for the spouses to recognize or admit to. These include the amount of time church leaders spend at church, on travel, and interacting with church members in private, as well as the level of trust spouses place in their husbands.

Because working for a mega-church involves a great deal of travel and private interaction with members and others outside the church, it is not difficult for church leaders to explain why they have been absent. For example, mega-church leaders conduct media interviews around the world, provide consultation to local and national leaders, and have constant business meetings to deal with church business. Spouses are not always allowed in many of these meetings. They cannot go along with their husbands on every trip. At the same time, working for a church is not like working in an office or other building complex. There are no boundaries as far as where church business is conducted. Some mega-church leaders travel the nation and even the world on a regular basis to visit satellite sites, operate missions in other countries, or attend conferences. Their office hours are not from nine to five, and they do not have five-day workweeks. When visiting missionaries in foreign nations, they may inaccessible by phone for days or even weeks.

The wives of mega-church ministers are like the wives of presidents, ambassadors, and chief executives. They must have extreme patience in sharing their spouse with thousands or millions of people. They have to trust their husbands are acting in the best interest of the church and their marriages when they are away from home.

The spouses of mega-church leaders are often busy as well. They attend and speak at conferences, give interviews, write books, are part of various clubs and organizations, and are engaged in business for the church that requires them to travel. Some of their positions are comparable to the first lady of the United States. Just as the president's wife has projects she personally sponsors and oversees, the "first ladies" of mega-churches are also intimately involved in their own projects. This is in addition to running their personal households and raising their children. Because of her own hectic schedule, a spouse may not recognize the signs of a cheating husband.

Some spouses are aware of warning signs that their church leader husband is cheating but try to ignore them. This is foremost because their husbands are ministers who have supposedly devoted their lives to their faith and their careers. Just like other members of the church, spouses have trusted their own faiths and devotion to the teachings of their husbands, who are also their ministers. Spouses dismiss warning signs of infidelity such as anxiousness, restlessness, and inattention as results of work stress. They view long trips, private meetings, and home visits with church members as part of a minister's work. Even suspicious phone calls made late at night are thought to be part of church business, given a minister with such a large membership is never "off-duty." Members may call with emergencies during any time of the day or night with problems including marital woes, themselves or family members being in trouble, or seeking advice. Because mega-churches have satellite locations, sometimes all over the world, time differences sometimes require calls during odd hours.

In other cases, spouses do confront their husbands on suspicions of infidelity but are persuaded to ignore their suspicions. Just as in normal marriages, the husband immediately retorts to any accusations by their spouse that their suspicions are based on paranoia and insecurity. There is also the defense of inflicting guilt through questioning by the minister as to how their spouse could levy such accusations given the good works and continuous labor the minister devotes toward the church and the sacrifices he faces in supporting his church and family. When the truth about a minister's actions is finally revealed, the pain endured by the spouse is that much greater given the times he adamantly denied her allegations.

The wives of very successful men often do not confront their husbands with suspicious or confirmed infidelity because they may perceive their husbands' actions as a failing in themselves. The wife will analyze what she did, or more likely did not do, to give him the support that he needed. She will question how she looks, dresses, acts in public, and their sex life. All of this is done in an attempt to pinpoint the primary reasons she may have driven her husband into the arms of someone else. Women, moreso than men, will blame themselves for such reasons as becoming unattractive after having a child, gaining weight, or changes to their looks as they grow older. This is often the case in those with issues related to low self-esteem. When women confront their cheating husbands, the questions of "What did I do wrong?" inevitably arise. Unfortunately, this may lead the cheating husband to take advantage of the situation presented and actually blame the spouse. It is important to point out that the husband has had an extremely successful career through persuading others to follow him. He is an expert negotiator, communicator, and persuader. Some are just as skilled at verbal and mental manipulation. The wife of a cheating mega-church minister faces a daunting task seeking a confession from a husband who does not want to volunteer one.

There are warning signs of infidelity, regardless of whether the cheating spouse is a church leader or someone working a normal job. Spouses and partners of suspected cheaters should not dismiss these signs as a "passing phase" if they persist or get worse. These signs include the following:

- Changing eating and sleeping patterns
- Lack of interest in sex
- Making excuses for coming home late such as being too drunk to drive or having car problems
- Frequently picking fights as an excuse to storm out and stay gone for long periods of time
- During arguments, talking about breaking up
- Long periods of moodiness or silence
- Wearing a different style of clothes
- Starting arguments or becoming very passive
- Working longer or different hours
- Unexplained phone calls during early morning or late at night
- Turning the table and accusing the noncheating spouse of infidelity
- Lessening or eliminating intimacy
- Growing inattention to the marriage, home, and family
- Pulling away from church and extended family
- Taking more showers than usual
- Comparing his spouse to other people

- Hiding credit card charges and cash withdrawals
- Taking off his wedding ring

For church leaders, the warnings signs may even be more specific and include the following:

- Taking long or frequent trips without clear explanations of where or why
- Taking long or frequent trips with unusual traveling companions such as young secretaries, minors, or persons not affiliated with the church, or often traveling alone
- Not discussing the details of trips with spouse, even when asked
- Not discussing the details of trips during sermons, or with church members or staff, especially when asked
- Conducting phone calls with persons the spouse is not aware of, such as nonchurch members, and calls in which the minister must leave the room to hold a private conversation
- Conducting phone calls in which the caller suddenly hangs up when the spouse answers the phone
- Being unwilling to share financial information, credit card receipts, details of itineraries, or access to computers or cell phones
- Being more attentive to his spouse than usual, especially during church service and with public praise of support and thankfulness for being a loyal companion
- Buying his spouse expensive gifts, particularly when returning from trips
- Constantly criticizing a particular person or group of people
- Criticizing or picking on how his spouse looks, dresses, or acts
- A sudden lack of in attentiveness to duties as church leader
- His spouse noticing strange looks from members and staff of the church
- His spouse noticing unusual people on the church payroll or performing church duties that they are not trained for or not the right age for
- His spouse noticing unusual people on the church payroll but never seeing them performing duties (or being paid an exorbitant amount of money for the duties they do perform)

Another troubling issue is when mega-church leaders commit acts of sexual misconduct and do so with the knowledge or support of their spouse. In cases of embezzlement, fiscal mismanagement, and other financial crimes, it may not be surprising that spouses support or act as accomplices of church leaders. They often reap the benefits of his misdeeds. However, some may be surprised the same is true in cases of sexual misconduct, even when minors or those of the same sex are the victims or sexual partners of male church leaders. Because of the large amounts of money mega-church leaders earn from their ministry, books, and speaking engagements, spouses sometimes turn a blind eye to their wrongdoings. This is true of spouses and partners of very rich people in countless professions. They are willing to accept the indiscretions being committed in order to continue reaping the benefits of wealth, power, and fame. Some wait until the affair has gone public before taking such actions as separation or divorce. However, they may do so then only out of public shame. Some even stay after this has happened.

There are other instances when the wife, other family members, or close friends of the perpetrator are aware of what is going on but take no action to try to stop it. In this case, they are codependents of the offender. For example, they may be aware of the perpetrator's cycle of sexual abuse of children yet do not intervene. There are many reasons people are codependent. They may suffer from low self-esteem, have been abused as children themselves, mentally detach themselves from reality, or have such high regard for the perpetrator that they just remain silent. In some cases, they are so in love with their spouse that they just will not do anything to jeopardize their relationship.

According to Mental Health America, codependency can affect the spouse, parent, sibling, friend, or coworker of a person with an addiction to sex, work, drugs, alcohol, relationships, or gambling. It also exists in families suffering from physical, emotional, or sexual abuse, as well as in situations in which a family member is suffering from a chronic mental or physical illness. The following are characteristics of a codependent person:[21]

- An exaggerated sense of responsibility for the actions of others
- A tendency to confuse love and pity with the tendency to "love" people one can pity and rescue
- A tendency to do more than one's share, all of the time
- A tendency to become hurt when people do not recognize one's efforts
- An unhealthy dependence on relationships; to avoid feeling abandoned, the codependent will do anything to hold on to a relationship
- An extreme need for approval and recognition
- A sense of guilt when asserting oneself
- A compelling need to control others
- Lack of trust in self and/or others

- Fear of being abandoned or alone
- Difficulty identifying feelings
- Rigidity/difficulty adjusting to change
- Problems with intimacy/boundaries
- Chronic anger
- Lying/dishonesty
- Poor communications
- Difficulty making decisions

What makes it even more difficult for a codependent person is not being able to seek help and having to hide one's problems from friends, family, coworkers, and others. This is the case for spouses of ministers. They often cannot seek counseling out of fear of their spouse's actions or family issues being made public. They have to go about their daily lives pretending everything is fine with them and their family. "Keeping up appearances" becomes a daunting task while they try to hide their true pain and suffering from public eyes. Their codependency drives them to try to hold onto their marriage by any means they can, including hiding their problems and inner pain. They lie for their spouse, help covering up his indiscretions, and make excuses for his behavior. With all of this comes a tremendous feeling of guilt for their behavior. They also have these feelings for allowing their lives to become consumed in supporting their spouse. Feelings of embarrassment, shame, and anger are constantly intertwined.

The codependency does not end until the person completely removes herself from the situation or the person on whom they are dependent completely cures himself of his addiction. This will often take both parties seeking counseling or medical attention. But it will still be years before both are fully cured.

In other situations, the wife knows about her husband but does not take action for reasons other than greed or codependence. Some do it for the sake of their small children. For example, a wife might decide to silently live with the knowledge of her husband's infidelity rather than put her children through a public divorce or end up having negative feelings toward their father. In other instances, the wife has nowhere to go. She may have signed a prenuptial agreement and does not have the financial means or family support to leave. The wife may also sincerely love her husband and not want to leave him. She holds on to the hope that he will eventually stop his behavior. Last, the wife may be traumatized. The knowledge that her husband has been abusing minors or frequenting prostitutes could leave her numb. She may withdraw from her husband, family members, and reality. She is just not able to cope with the situation.

Chapter 5

Implications for Society: Bad Actions Breed Discontent

The debate over the ability of mega-churches to serve the needs of their membership is based on the large size of these entities and their being led primarily under the leadership of a single person. Although they exist as primarily independent entities, they have the same characteristics as organized religious organizations with a hierarchical structure. The Roman Catholic Church operates under the leadership of a single pope who is supported by bishops. Mega-churches have a single leader who is supported by assistant ministers. Mega-churches also expand with satellite campuses throughout the nation and in some cases throughout the world. The most interesting point here is that mega-churches evolve into the very structure that they grew into popularity as an alternative to—an organized structure of religious worship based upon hierarchical operation. There is no argument over the good these churches do in filling a gap that exists in American religion. Due to the array of religious services mega-churches provide, they allow members to worship based upon their individual religious preferences. However, their collective goodness is tainted by the huge shadow sexual misconduct by their leaders exerts on society's view of mega-churches and organized religion.

Results from a recent Gallup poll show sexual misconduct in churches has had a negative impact on society's general view of religion. The survey shows that in 2012, the confidence Americans have in organized religion reached an all time low. Only 45 percent of responders had a "great deal" or "lot of confidence" in churches and organized religions. This followed a decline in confidence that began in 1973. The decline was reported to be possibly due to sex scandals in both mega-churches and the Roman Catholic Church. As outlined in the report,

> In 1973, "the church or organized religion" was the most highly rated institution in Gallup's confidence in institutions measure, and it continued to rank first in most years through 1985, outranking the military and the U.S. Supreme Court, among others. That began to change in the mid to late 1980s as confidence in organized religion first fell below 60 percent, possibly resulting from scandals during that time involving famed televangelist preachers Jim Bakker and Jimmy Swaggart. Confidence in religion returned to 60 percent in 2001, only to be rocked the following year by charges of child molestation by Catholic priests and cover-up by some in the church.[1]

This pointing to mega-churches as part of the problem is a major issue. While the Roman Catholic Church has been in existence for centuries, mega-churches have existed for only a few decades. However, sexual scandals in mega-churches having such an impact underscores their influence and the great damage sexual misconduct by their leaders has on society.

The influence of mega-churches is a direct result of their leaders. The reputation of the church and particularly its leader are the primary reasons new and old members alike attend mega-churches. A survey of almost 25,000 responders conducted by Thumma and Bird found that "what first attracted attenders were the worship style, the senior pastor and the church's reputation. These same factors also influenced long-term attendance, as did the music/arts, social and community outreach and adult-oriented programs."[2] An act of sexual misconduct drives members from the church. In some cases, they find other churches. In other cases, they give up attending church all together. They become so disillusioned by the event in their current church and by reports of similar misconduct in others that they believe all churches are all corrupt. For some people, such scandals negatively impact their overall view of religion. Others may maintain their religious or spiritual belief but lose faith in churches being able to provide support consistent with their beliefs. This is especially true of young people who are involved in or aware of misdeeds taking place. They will just stop going to church.

Even discounting sex scandals, the value of mega-churches is already heavily debated. They are praised by many, but also heavily criticized by others. For example, many criticize them for distorting Christianity in favor of attracting large memberships. As Douthat discussed in *Bad Religion: How We Became a Nation of Heretics*,

The United States remains a deeply religious country, and most Americans are still drawing some water from the Christian well. But a growing number are inventing their own versions of what Christianity means, abandoning the nuances of traditional theology in favor of religions that stroke their egos and indulge or even celebrate their worst impulses. These faiths speak from many pulpits—conservative and liberal, political and pop-cultural, traditionally religious and fashionably spiritual—and many of their preachers call themselves Christian or claim a Christian warrant. But they are increasingly offering distortions of traditional Christianity, not the real thing.[3]

The preceding quotation particularly speaks to how mega-churches are viewed by many, both supporters and critics. These churches thrive on glitz and entertainment to attract members. Their ideological practice is based upon abandoning structured theology in order to speak to the individual needs and wants of members. They even justify some indulgences and impulses such as becoming wealthier and living an extravagant life. As will be discussed later, many preach what has been called the prosperity ministry. The extravagant lifestyles of mega-church leaders speak to their belief in acquiring material wealth. Some go so far as to justify and encourage personal pleasure. Ed Young, pastor of the Fellowship Church in Grapevine, Texas, shocked some members and caused national controversy when he gave a sermon urging the married couples in his congregation to have more sex. He spoke on the importance of sex for married Christians and asked each couple to have sex each day for one week. He then went so far as to plan a 24-hour "Sexperiment" in 2012 in which he and his wife would spend 24 hours on the roof of the church in bed. They would not be having sex, but would be holding bedside interviews with members through Skype to answer intimacy questions. Young and his wife published a book on the topic, also entitled *Sexperiment*. This was not the first time Young caused national controversy.[4] In 2010, he urged his members to give the church their banking account and routing numbers so that their tithes could be automatically withdrawn.

Many also consider mega-churches somewhat of a religious fad and contemplate if and how long they will remain a permanent fixture of American culture. Those in favor of mega-churches insist they will forever change how Americans worship and praise their ability to make religion popular again, especially instilling religious vigor in youth. Renowned management consultant and author Peter Drucker stated, "The most significant sociological phenomenon of the first half of the 20th century was the rise of the corporation. The most significant sociological phenomenon of the second half of the 20th century has been the development of the large pastoral church—of the mega-church. It is the only organization that is actually working in our society."[5] Drucker made this statement because he viewed the management style of mega-churches as effective and efficient, and praised their ability to meet the needs of their customers, that is, their members.

Mega-church services are designed to excite and inspire members with music, lighting, and emotion. At the same time, religious messages are presented in a way that people can relate lessons to ordinary lives. Sermons are presented using modern idioms that draw on the daily concerns and issues that everyday people face. The churches reflect society because their memberships are comprised of people of different sexes, ages, and races.

Mega-churches are also hailed for supporting their local communities with much needed social and community development programs, scholarships for youths, and assistance in times of disasters. These churches assist both church members and nonmembers within and outside of the local community. They build homes for the poor, provide prison ministries, give food to the homeless, provide local jobs, and sponsor programs to assist senior citizens. During hurricane Katrina, for example, mega-churches mobilized their members to support displaced victims with food, shelter and medicine. For example, over 3,000 members of Joel Osteen's Lakewood Church volunteered at shelters in conjunction with volunteers from other churches to distribute supplies to victims.[6]

As stated earlier in this chapter, mega-churches are also seen as positive forces in the United States because they have revitalized religion in U.S. culture. Mainline religions have experienced reduced memberships and lack of interest by young people because of their unwavering and condemning theologies. Their strict stance on such issues as abortion, homosexuality, and single parenting seems out of place and out of touch with modern values and practices. At the same time they shun the media from getting involved in their inner workings, they attempt to aggressively impact politics. For example, in 2012, the pastor of Grace Community Church in Texas asked the mayor of Houston, Annise Parker, to step down because of her support of same-sex marriage. Pastor Steve Riggle made this demand based upon his view that the mayor was not upholding the state's constitution. During a sermon, he quoted the state's law defining marriage as being between one man and one woman, and sent a letter to the mayor asking her to resign if she did not change her stance. Parker is the nation's first openly gay mayor of a major U.S. city and joined other mayors during the U.S. Conference of Mayors in Washington, D.C., in January 2012 calling for the legalization of same-sex marriage.

Many in society view mega-churches negatively. They are criticized for being large entities that first steal members from other churches and then are unable to meet the spiritual needs of so many members. Due to their size, they have been called McChurches and big box churches because they are organized under a central operating base with branch or satellite campuses. Just as businesses do, mega-churches employ advertising campaigns, market surveys, and polls to help them increase their membership and reach their target market of young, affluent professionals. Some churches judge their success by their size rather than their ability to meet members' spiritual needs.

Mega-churches are unique in that they each were generally started as entities that were different or better than existing churches and organized religions. In this sense, they were founded based on criticizing existing churches for being stolid and out of touch with modern times, and thus unable to meet the spiritual needs of society. Many members of mega-church were formerly members of other churches, leading to a criticism that mega-churches steal their members from other churches. That is why they are characterized as "seeker" churches. Not only do they target or seek those who attend no churches at all, but they also target those who are seeking a new religious experience their current church does not offer. Therefore, there already exists a suspicion that mega-churches are really interested in boosting their memberships through deceit.

Because of their size, they generate a huge amount of income. According to a report in *Businessweek*, "All this growth, plus the tithing many evangelicals encourage, is generating gushers of cash. A traditional U.S. church typically has fewer than 200 members and an annual budget of around $100,000. The average mega-church pulls in $4.8 million, according to a 1999 study by the Hartford Seminary, one of the few surveys on the topic. The money is also fueling a mega-church building boom. First Baptist Church of Woodstock, near Atlanta, for example, has just finished a $62 million, 7,000-seat sanctuary."[7]

The finances of mega-churches have caused the greatest criticisms, and particularly the lack of outside oversight of how the money is being spent. According to an article by Goh in *Material Religion*, "One of the biggest points of criticism and thus one of the main divisive issues associated with mega-churches, is that of finances: not just the amount of money involved in mega-church operations, but also the structures of revenue-gathering and accountability (or the lack thereof) associated with those operations. Ferguson sums up many of the Christian criticisms of mega-church finances: their 'tax breaks' and government grants which give them a 'big advantage over the commercial world,' their 'lack of accountability' in finances, the cult of 'multi-millionaire' pastors and related features."[8]

Because mega-churches are nonprofit tax-exempt entities, there are additional concerns over how they spend the money they raise. Unlike charitable organizations that have to file financial statements detailing how they spend donated funds, churches are not required to. Their spending is kept internal to the church and often not revealed even to its members. In smaller churches, members are able to have some oversight of funds because the primary source of revenue for the church is member donations. With so little money, it is not difficult to discern how much is being raised, and church meetings are often attended by the majority of church members. During these meetings, church finances are a primary topic, and areas of spending are voted on.

Mega-churches, however, have so many members that only a select few are invited to church meetings. Additionally, the sources of revenues are diverse. Funds are raised from resident church members, members who may be located around the world, foundations, and nonmember donators. Thousands and sometimes millions of dollars are raised each week. Consider televangelists. They have an unlimited supply of donors from around the world, and the tracking of donations by outside parties is virtually impossible. Church leaders have great liberty to access church funds. Beyond their salaries (and even for those who do not accept salaries), mega-church leaders have access to funds for lavish trips, personal expenses, and varied categories of "business expenses." This not only includes access to cash, but also use of credit cards paid for by the church. Many mega-church leaders also place friends and relatives on the church payroll. This gives leaders even more access to church funds under the guise of legitimacy. While ministers' salaries are taxable, some mega-church leaders do not accept salaries. This allows them to pay no taxes but spend church funds and claim the spending as church business expenses.

A number of mega-church leaders have been convicted of embezzlement and using church funds for their personal benefit, and other ministers and churches have been investigated for spending money illegally, for example, supporting political candidates' campaigns. Many outside of these churches question whether mega-churches should maintain their tax-exempt status given all of these factors. As churches, they are not required to disclose their incomes to the government because they are classified as nonprofit entities, so it nearly impossible to know how much money they actually take in.

Churches also provide a housing allowance for church leaders, even those who do not receive salaries. Ministers do not have to claim the rental values of their homes as taxable income. Although many critics agree there is a need for greater governmental regulation of mega-churches and other large religious organizations, this is unlikely due to the separation of church and state as well as the unwillingness of politicians to take a strong stance against religion due to the voters possibly viewing their actions in a negative light. With so many members, mega-churches have a large amount of political clout. Ministers are sometimes vocal about their opinion of political decisions and can sway members on which political candidate to support or oppose because of their stances on certain issues.

The United States was founded based partly upon the principle of separation of church and state. This was done to prevent the government from infringing upon or controlling citizens' religious beliefs and practices. However, evangelical mega-churches have been criticized for infringing upon government practices through political influence. Presidents such as George W. Bush and members of Congress identify themselves as evangelicals. Mega-church leaders rally members to influence politics, and politicians frequent these churches when attempting to rally support for new legislation. In the 1980s, Jerry Falwell formed the Moral Majority to influence political decision making based upon evangelical philosophy.

The criticism of the size of mega-churches was aptly characterized by Lyle Schaller in an article in *Christianity Today*:

The rapid growth of the mega-churches has aroused a host of critics. Most of their criticisms center on problems generally associated with size. The most repeated—and misunderstood—criticism is obvious: the mega-church is a more-expensive operation. In most very large congregations, annual expenditures run between $1,000 to $1,500 per person (average worship attendance). In a few, expenses run as high as $2,000 to $4,000 per person when the costs of a pay-as-you-go building program are included. By contrast, in most small churches, annual expenditures average out to between $400 and $600 per person, while in middle-size congregations that average usually is between $700 and $1,500 . . . Another problem for mega-churches is that anonymity and complexity go up as size increases. Those who prefer an intimate and friendly atmosphere in which everyone can call every other member by name often find the mega-church overwhelming. Most mega-churches try to compensate for this by structuring themselves as a congregation of congregations, classes, groups, cells, and fellowships. Most of the caring is carried out in and through these smaller clusters of people. Apparently the majority of the adults in mega-churches are willing to accept anonymity and complexity in exchange for choices and quality.[9]

Mega-churches are also criticized for abandoning the unique histories, theology, and culture of their religions through the modernization of their worship services, which resemble secular entertainment venues. Church services include elaborate visual productions, rock-and-roll or rhythm-and-blues music, step shows, and dancers. These are all used as modern forms of worship to target youth members. Many feel these churches are more focused on entertainment than delivering a message. Some refer to this as the Disneyfication of religion, meaning the weakening of the church's theological message to the point that attending services is for entertainment rather than spiritual growth. In conjunction with this is the feeling by some that these churches have a cult-like quality in how they conduct their services.

As stated earlier, another major criticism is how mega-church leaders publicly speak on the goodness of having material wealth. They credit their faith and good works for their extremely high incomes, large houses, and fashionable dress. Some own private jets, drive such elaborate cars as Rolls Royces and Bentleys, and live in multi-million dollar homes on huge estates. Their belief in being elaborate is evidenced in the décor of their churches. For example, Kenneth Copeland founded a ministry that is named after him (Kenneth Copeland Ministries). Paid for from donations to his ministry, he flies on private jets out of Kenneth Copeland Airport in Fort Worth, Texas. This is a far cry from traditional religious teachings of the sins of excess. Creflo Dollar, leader of World Changers International Church in Fulton County, Georgia, preaches that wealth is a blessing and that God does not want people to be poor. He defends his driving two Rolls Royces as a gift from his church. He also owns a private jet, a million dollar home in Atlanta and a $2.5 million home in Manhattan.

Like some other mega-church leaders, Dollar has refused to disclose his salary to the general public and even to Congress during a Senate probe of his and other mega-church leaders' lavish lifestyles. The probe was launched in 2007 by Senator Chuck Grassley of Iowa to determine if church leaders were using church donations for personal profit and if their lavish lifestyles violated their churches' tax-exempt status. In addition to requesting financial information from Copeland and Dollar, the probe also requested information from other mega-church leaders: Benny Hinn, T. D. Jakes, Eddie Long, Joyce Meyer, and Paula White. Only Hinn and Meyer fully participated in the probe, and both committed to instituting financial reforms in their ministries. The following are examples of some of the excessive spending items that were specifically investigated by the probe:[10]

- Information about the use of the church's private jet, reportedly a $20 million Cessna, used by Copeland for layovers and trips, many of which were personal vacations taken with friends.
- Compensation, including cash, housing allowances, loans, and personal use of jets, employees, and facilities by Dollar. Also details of monthly expenses for Dollar's residences, including those in Georgia and New York.

- Statements for all credit cards used by Hinn and family members, particularly when expenses were paid by the church. Additional details about how payments were made for Hinn's clothing, jewelry, and personal grooming.
- Information about a home purchased by the nonprofit Bishop Eddie Long Ministries for Long's personal use, as well his Bentley automobile, which was also paid for by his charity organization.
- Detailed explanation of credit card expenses for such items as clothing and cosmetic surgery for the Whites that were paid for by the church. Also details of how the purchase and maintenance of the family's homes in San Antonio, Texas; Malibu, California; and New York City.
- A copy of the bill of sale and payment method for a Bentley convertible purchased for T. D. Jakes.

In addition to all of these concerns are the many incidents of mega-church leaders having sexual affairs, molesting children, committing sexual assault, soliciting prostitutes, and other acts of sexual misconduct. This adds to questions about the credibility of mega-churches and the necessity for their continued existence. This questioning is then applied to organized religion, institutionalized religions, and large church entities in general. Religion in the United States is already fluid. According to studies conducted by the Pew Research Center, Trinity College, and the U.S. Census Bureau, in 2008, approximately 15 percent of Americans indentified themselves has having no religious affiliation. This population includes those that were atheist, agnostic, humanist, or just did not have a religion. This percentage can be compared to approximately 8 percent in 1990 and 14.1 percent in 2001. Of the nonbelievers in 2008, 24 percent were between 18 and 24 years of age, and 41 percent were between 30 and 49, with both age groups accounting for 70 percent of adult nonbelievers.[11] Major scandals in mega-churches coupled with those in major religions have contributed to growing numbers of nonbelievers. A lack of religion impacts more than just a person attending church. It has a negative impact on the likelihood of a person voting, giving to charities, and performing volunteer work. A lack of religion has been theorized to cause increased crime rates, infidelity, sexual promiscuity, and suicide. A lack of faith also contributes to increased stress without the coping support religion provides.

A growing lack of religion also raises philosophical questions about Americans and particularly youth. Religion has served as the foundation for establishing standards of morality and ethics. It is the cornerstone of individual and social values that has established the cultures of virtually all civilizations. Without some sense of religion to serve as an ethical compass, some may have ethical norms that are completely out of skew with those in their community and with society in general. There are many arguments about whether morality can exist without religion. However, a lack of religion means a person must rely on secular codes of conduct to determine right and wrong. Therefore, their actions are driven by behavior derived from members of their community and from such sources as entertainment, music, and movies. Based upon this premise, one's behavior could be harmful to oneself and others if one is negatively influenced. Dixon speaks to this line of reasoning in *Science and Religion: A Very Short Introduction*:[12]

When freethinking and anti-Christian works such as Thomas Paine's *Age of Reason* (1794) started to become more widely available, one of the leading concerns of the faithful was that if people ceased to believe in heaven and hell, then they would feel free to indulge their most sensual passions and selfish appetites. Without religion, it was feared, human society would descend into animalistic anarchy. As one judge said when sentencing a London bookseller to imprisonment for selling Paine's works, if these books were widely read and believed then the law would be deprived of one of its principal sanctions—the dread of future punishments.

Many today still echo the sentiments of this 18th-century judge and argue that religious beliefs are necessary to provide moral guidance and standards of virtuous conduct in an otherwise corrupt, materialistic, and degenerate world. Religions certainly do provide a framework within which people can learn the difference between right and wrong. An individual might consult the scriptures to discover that God had told his people to be truthful, faithful, and respectful towards their parents; and not to steal, nor commit adultery, nor worship false gods. Believers can also hope to receive moral guidance from the voice of God within, in the form of their conscience. If they follow the divine path faithfully, they will be deemed to be among the righteous rather than the wicked at the day of judgment. The unbeliever, in contrast, is supposed to be a sensuous, self-indulgent, selfish creature whose motto is "Let us eat and drink; for tomorrow we die."

Other researchers and theorists find that a decline in religion not only impacts the individual, but also leads to the moral and ethical decline of families, governments, and other institutions within the society. As Hunt discussed in *Religion and Everyday Life*,

The apparent decline of civil religion in Western societies as a broad and loose form of religious socialization and means of social integration has been noted for its negative consequences. In exploring links between the decline of religion and moral decay, Anthony and Robbins list some of the negative consequences for Western society, particularly for the USA. These include a crisis of moral meaning and boundaries leading to uncertainties in basic guidelines of behavior, e.g., sexual permissiveness, lack of faith in traditional social and political institutions, the internal dysfunctioning of these institutions—perhaps displayed in corruption in government, increase in the divorce rate and family disintegration, rising crime and shrinking voting turnouts. While the attempt to establish a link between declining civil religions and morality may constitute something of a tautology, evidence of the decline of shared religious commonality is certainly evident.[13]

Along this line of cause-and-effect reasoning, societal effects include bad decision making and unacceptable behaviors by government officials, politicians, police officers, judges, teachers, lawyers, and others charged with serving the public good. Their actions are based on the downfall of religious leaders, who serve as the religious and moral foundation and example for most every society and culture.

The other side of this debate is the argument that people can still be moral even if they are atheists. As Baggini argues in *Atheism: A Very Short Introduction*, "Morality is more than possible without God, it is entirely independent of him. That means atheists are not only more than capable of leading moral lives, they may even be able to lead more moral lives than religious believers who confuse divine law and punishment with right and wrong. These conclusions run counter to much received wisdom, but the arguments that lead to them are reasonably clear and straightforward."[14] He goes further by comparing people needing religion to be moral to people needing a legal system to obey laws: "Law certainly does require a legislature and judiciary. But the existence of both does not guarantee that the laws enacted and enforced will be just and good laws. One can have immoral laws as well as moral ones. What is required for just laws is for the legislature and judiciary to act within the confines of morality. Morality is thus separate from law. It is the basis upon which just laws are enacted and enforced; it is not constituted by the law themselves."[15]

Last, a recent study published in *Child Psychiatry & Human Development* conducted a review of the literature on religion and spirituality as it pertains to adolescent psychiatric symptoms. From the review, "One hundred and fifteen articles were reviewed that examined relationships between religion/spirituality and adolescent substance use, delinquency, depression, suicidality, and anxiety. Ninety-two percent of articles reviewed found at least one significant ($p < .05$) relationship between religiousness and better mental health. Evidence for relationships between greater religiousness and less psychopathology was strongest in the area of teenage substance use."[16]

When mega-church leaders and others religious leaders act inappropriately, it leads more people with religion to question their faith. Those who are questioning their faith may turn from religion all together. It also causes others to commit the same acts and justify their behavior by the religious leader's example. Since ministers are held as the pinnacle of faith and fortitude in most societies and cultures, regular people will feel none can be trusted. However, ministers' level of regard in U.S. society is steadily declining. When acts of ministerial sexual misconduct are made public today, many people are just not surprised. These acts are almost expected of ministers. Most media reports about ministerial sexual misconduct, now begin with, "Another ... minister [or priest] has been charged ... "

Thousands of ministers, pastors, and priests are firmly committed to their faith and their chosen mission. They spend their lives both preaching and living a devout life, including being faithful to their families. Catholic priests, mega-church leaders, and those from other faiths who engage in acts of sexual misconduct taint the image of all church leaders and religious entities in general. This is analogous to the view that all politicians are crooked due to the actions of a few who have committed crimes. Trust and respect are the two factors that religious leaders most rely on to successfully perform their missions. A loss of either due to their actions or the actions of others is detrimental not only to themselves and their churches, but to society's overall view of religion. Studies conducted after sex scandals exemplify how congregation members' trust plummets. A study by Mark Chaves discussed in *American Religion: Contemporary Trends* found that Americans have lost confidence in religious leaders. Based upon data from the General Social Survey and the National Congregations Study, he found that the percentage of people with "great confidence" in religious leaders declined from 35 percent to less than 25 percent between 1973 and 2008.[17]

Chapter 6

How to End the Suffering: Strategies to End Sexual Misconduct in Mega-Churches

Proactively addressing sexual misconduct in the church is analogous to buying earthquake insurance. It is something that may occur in the future, but not something people think will ever happen. If it does, actions will be taken to address it at that time. However, the damage to the church can be extensive. It is also hard to proactively address given the taboo subject of sex in the church. This is especially true in discussing infidelity and sex outside of marriage. In professional settings, sexual harassment and employee fraternization are common topics of employee orientation and training. Although mega-churches act like businesses in terms of how they are operate and market themselves, they have yet to adopt practices that conflict with general religious ideology such as proactively preparing for instances of sexual misconduct.

Perhaps there is no way to ever fully end incidents of sexual misconduct by religious leaders, just as there is no way to end rape and molestation in the general public. Sexual misconduct has taken place for centuries in the Roman Catholic Church, other denominations, and by religious leaders not affiliated with any formally organized religion. Incidents by leaders of mega-churches occur for the same reasons: lack of oversight by church leaders, lack of accountability by ministers, blind trust by church members, and fear by some victims and participatory willingness in others.

However, things can be done to curb the number of incidents and stop culprits before they become repetitive offenders.

Dallas and Heche wrote on several studies that have revealed the prevalence of sexual misconduct in American churches in *The Complete Christian Guide to Understanding Homosexuality: A Biblical and Compassionate Response to Same-Sex Attraction*. They discussed a survey in the *Journal of Pastoral Care* of 1,000 senior Southern Baptist pastors who were randomly selected from 15,000 churches. Fourteen percent acknowledged they had engaged in "sexual behavior inappropriate to a minister." The 1993 study also reported 70 percent had counseled at least one woman who had engaged in sex with another minister. In a survey conducted by *Christianity Today* in 2000, "33 percent of clergy admitted to having visited a sexually explicit website. Of those who had visited a porn site, 53 percent had visited such sites a few times in the past year, and 18 percent had visited sexually explicit sites between a couple of times a month and more than once a week."[1]

A 1997 *Newsweek* article reported that "various surveys suggested that as many as 30 percent of male Protestant ministers had had sexual relationships with women other than their wives." The same article continued to report that

In 1988 a survey of nearly 1,000 Protestant clergy by *Leadership* magazine found that 12 percent admitted to sexual intercourse outside marriage. Seventeen percent of these affairs occurred with people they were counseling, and 52 percent involved members, ministers or other leaders of their own congregation. An additional 18 percent disclosed that they had kissed, fondled or masturbated with someone other than their spouse. When asked what consequences they had suffered—in their marriages or their careers—as a result of their sexual adventures, only 6 percent said that they had lost their jobs. And nearly a third reported no adverse consequences of any kind.[2]

The primary reason for sexual misconduct in mega-churches is blind trust. Schmitz explains this in *Staying in Bounds: Straight Talk on Boundaries for Effective Ministry*: "Perceived power is the level of deference or acquiescence to the pastor by the parishioners. Centuries of church history have led to a widespread notion that a 'good' Christian is characterized by submission to church leaders. As with any guidance taken to the extreme, indiscriminate and absolute submission is not healthy and can lead to trouble. Although it is the responsibility of the pastor to not misuse the power intrinsic to the position of spiritual leader, indiscriminate submission is possibly the biggest contribution by parishioners to creating opportunities for the misuse of power."[3]

Church members' trust feeds the power that these leaders exert to the point that they feel they can commit harmful acts and get away with them. For example, one wonders how church leaders have had access to children and minors to the point that they have committed sexual acts against them so many times. Where were the parents? Church members should exercise the same level of caution with church leaders as they would with an adult outside of the church. First, they should not allow their children to be alone with church leaders or taken on trips without parental supervision. Parents should also be cautious of changes in their children's behavior, aware of who they are talking to online and on the phone, always know their whereabouts, and use extreme caution if any adult or older child asks to spend time with their children alone. If a child does go on a church-sponsored trip without his or her parents, the parents should ask the same questions they would if their child were going on a school trip. These questions include where they are going on the trip, what the mode of transportation is, the names and phone numbers of all adults attending, a contact number for the person in charge of the trip, a contact number for the primary adult going on the trip, the name and numbers for any hotels being used, the dates of arrival and departure, and the date and time of return home. When the child returns, the parents should be adamant that the child disclose all details of the trip.

Special training should be required of anyone working with children. This includes counselors, instructors, and ministers. It should be given to those working in schools, day cares, before and after school programs, youth choir programs, social programs (such as the Boy Scouts), sports, and any event dealing with children. This training should not only address preventing situations where misconduct may take place, but also provide instruction on how to recognize signs of misconduct being perpetuated by others. Those trained should be required to sign a document outlining proper and improper codes of conduct. This document should stipulate what actions will result in dismissal and legal action being taken by the church. At the same time, there should be mandatory counseling required of those convicted of sexual acts. This is in line with the mission of the church to support its members, including ministers and others who are accused of wrongdoing. Counseling should also be offered to the church at large. There may be members of the church upset about the victim or the minister, or some may be upset over memories of similar experiences they have dealt that are rekindled by the incident.

Mega-churches must adopt a wide range of business practices when they grow, and not practices just based on attracting new members and raising money. They act just like profitable businesses in marketing, managing finances, conducting human resource functions, and providing services to their members and the community. Church members should ensure there is a system in place for reporting any misconduct by any member of the church, including the church leader. This system should be under the congregation's control, meaning the church leader does not have control or influence over the reporting process or how cases are handled. The church should even have an impartial legal staff that reports to a board consisting of church staff, parents, and community leaders. Many businesses, especially large ones, have processes for reporting ethical and business violations in a nonattribution environment that leads to an investigation of alleged charges.

Just as businesses do, churches must also establish sexual harassment policies. These policies should outline what is considered sexual harassment with examples, specify responsibilities of all members of and those associated with the church, and outline consequences for violations. If violations occur by church leaders, especially in the case of sexual misconduct, the church as a whole must take responsibility. The congregation should be told of the incident, and the church must take responsibility for providing support to the victim. The latter includes paying for legal and counseling costs. There should be clearly outlined steps for what actions will lead to the church leader's dismissal, such as sex with minors within and outside of the church.

For mega-churches, being proactive and serious about dealing with sexual misconduct includes forming a coalition with other churches, religious organizations, and nonreligious organizations dedicated to addressing sex abuse by ministers. For example, the Survivors Network of those Abused by Priests (SNAP) is an independent, confidential network of survivors of religious sexual abuse and their supporters who work to end sexual abuse. According to SNAP's website (www.snapnetwork.org), the organization builds policies and practices within secular and religious organizations that protect children now and in the future, shares stories of those that have been abused to assist others in healing, and exposes the malignant actions of abusive religious ministers and the church officials who shield them. It is one of many organizations that have battled against sex abuse in the Roman Catholic Church. However, the organization has expanded its focus to abuse by Baptist pastors. It seeks to develop a database of ministerial sex abusers across denominations. According David Clohessy, the organization's national director, "Baptist officials, we believe, need to compile a thorough, online database of proven, admitted and credibly accused pedophile clergy, so that kids can be protected and parents can be warned."[4] Supporting such organizations should be the duty of churches as well.

The Southern Baptist Convention has taken similar steps. It studied the feasibility of establishing such a database but did not due to the autonomy of churches and the inability to force reporting. This shows churches' defiance of such efforts. Still, the convention's website includes various resources to assist churches in developing programs to address sexual abuse, particularly abuse of children by ministers. The organization passed a resolution via "On the Sexual Integrity of Ministers" in June 2002 that includes following statements:

RESOLVED, That the messengers to the Southern Baptist Convention meeting in St. Louis, Missouri, June 11–12, 2002, call one another to build and maintain relationships and practices of integrity and fidelity to God and others; and be it further

RESOLVED, That we urge all our spiritual leaders to hold one another accountable to the highest standards of Christian moral practice; and be it further

RESOLVED, That we urge our seminaries and other related educational institutions to make ministerial integrity a major emphasis in the training of pastors, missionaries, educators, and other ministers; and be it further

RESOLVED, That we encourage those religious bodies dealing with the tragedy of clergy abuse in their efforts to rid their ranks of predatory ministers; and be it further

RESOLVED, That we call on civil authorities to punish to the fullest extent of the law sexual abuse among clergy and counselors; and be it further

RESOLVED, That we call on our churches to discipline those guilty of any sexual abuse in obedience to Matthew 18:6–17 as well as to cooperate with civil authorities in the prosecution of those cases; and be it finally

RESOLVED, That we pray for those who have been harmed as a result of sexual abuse and urge our churches to offer support, compassion, and biblical counseling to them and their families.

Organized religions are taking steps to change the culture of sexual abuse within their ranks. The Roman Catholic, Methodist, and Baptist churches, for example, are taking aggressive actions to establish policies, procedures, and programs to both prevent and deal with acts of sexual misconduct by their priests, pastors, and ministers. This is more difficult for mega-churches because they are not linked to one organized body of leadership. They are in this sense hampered by their individuality. However, regardless of whether a stance against sexual misconduct is taken by an organized religion or a single church, it will not succeed unless church leaders accept and practice the measures developed. Needless to say, this is difficult for mega-churches when the leader of the church holds complete or majority power and is also the person committing sexual misconduct. For this reason, the cultures of mega-churches must change to not allow one person to have complete control over the church. This is analogous to a major corporation. It may have begun as a small business started by one man or woman. However, the company reaches a point of success and size in which power is relinquished to shareholders. These shareholders rely on a board of directors to oversee the well-being of the company, and the business founder then serves as chief executive officer (CEO) or president. The CEO is held to rules and policies enforced by the board of directors, and—if they feel their interests are not being served—shareholders have the ability to elect a new CEO and board of directors. Mega-churches should operate under the same principle.

Any church-related travel should require a formal request and approval process, as well as a review of repayment of expenses via a voucher outlining all expenses incurred. Even trips paid from a minister's personal funds should be documented if church members attend. Written justification should be given for anyone traveling with the minister, with written permission gained from parents for any minors traveling.

Church leaders, staff members, and volunteers should be required to submit to a criminal background check and employment screenings. The latter may reveal issues that were not reported to law enforcement officials. These checks must be performed because these people are handling large sums of money, working closely with children, and working closely with church members who may have addictive behaviors or psychological problems. Pertinent information on their resumes should also be verified, for example, their education. Care must be taken that background checks and verification of any information is done fairly and per established practices. The type and scope of the review should be commensurate with the responsibilities and duties assigned. While a minister may be subject to a full background and credit check, the same may not be necessary for subordinates. For example, a credit check is not needed for a staff member who will not be involved with church finances.

Many methods can be used to conduct background checks on potential employees and volunteers. Churches can do these themselves, hire professionals such as investigators or firms that specialize in conducting checks, or use online companies that provide this service. The following is list of some of the primary methods of performing background checks:

- Employment reference checks
- Personal reference checks
- Personal interviews
- Confirmation of education
- Written application
- On-the-job observation
- Check social networking sites
- Local criminal record check
- State criminal record check

- Federal Bureau of Investigation (FBI) criminal record check
- State central child and dependent adult abuse registry check
- State sex offender registry check
- Nurse's aide registry record check
- Motor vehicle record check
- Professional disciplinary board background check
- Verification of education and certifications
- Alcohol and drug testing
- Psychological testing
- Mental illness and psychiatric history check
- Home visits

Federal laws allow private organizations and businesses to conduct background checks on people working with children. Both paid employees and volunteers can be screened. The National Child Protection Act was passed 1993 (and signed by President Bill Clinton) to allow schools, day cares, and other organizations working with youths access to a nationwide fingerprint criminal database. However, the act required states to submit the information and enact individual statutes to establish additional legislation to address "qualified entities" that had to comply. A qualified entity is any business or organization that provides care, treatment, education, training, instruction, supervision, or recreation for children, older adults, or individuals with disabilities. This includes public, private, for-profit, nonprofit, and voluntary businesses and organizations. Entities cannot access federal background information on potential applicants unless their state has issued a law allowing them to. Because some states did not comply with the federal act and doing so would create an extra burden on them, Congress passed the Volunteers for Children Act of 1998. This new law gave these qualified entities direct access to the FBI database outlining nationwide individual criminal histories. The system is based on fingerprinting, so even individuals who have changed their names, obtained new social security numbers, or moved to a state different from where their crime was committed can be identified. State laws still define qualified entities, so churches have to check with the state's attorney general or other authorizing office to ensure they are allowed access. The database can be used not only for those working with children, but also for those working with older adults and people with disabilities.

Within each organization, consideration must also be given to the type of disparate information that could cause a person to be rejected from consideration for a job. For example, a person convicted of a crime many years ago should not be disqualified if it can be shown he has been fully rehabilitated. If any disparate information is revealed, the applicant must be notified of the exact nature of the information and be given ample time to respond. It is not uncommon for information to be false or for the applicant to provide a justification that adequately explains what actions he has taken to rectify past failings. In all cases, care must also be taken to ensure personal information obtained is held within the strictest of confidence. Information should be revealed on a need-to-know basis, namely only to those directly involved in the hiring process. Personal information must be handled according to state and federal law. Churches cannot obtain information held by state and local agencies and then feel they have the right to ignore the policies and laws that govern its use. Of course, some information requires full disclosure. Those who are convicted child abusers, for example, must publicly disclose this to anyone impacted by their potential contact with children.

Once hired, ministers, staff, and even volunteers should be required to sign contracts or other documentation outlining expected standards of ethical behavior. This documentation should also outline consequences for misconduct and stipulate the types of sexual misconduct that will be disclosed to law enforcement officials (e.g., sex with a minor, rape). Each person should be given complete job descriptions outlining duties and responsibilities, and there should be clear lines of supervision whereby performance evaluations are regularly conducted.

The Alabama Baptist Convention State Board of Missions has published extensive material on this topic, including "Preventing Sexual Misconduct in Your Church."[5] In this document, they provide many recommendations. For example, the following are recommended actions to take when churches are considering hiring a staff member, including a minister, director, or coordinator:

- Check references (those that are listed and not those that are not listed), including directors of missions, former staff members that have worked with the candidate, and church and community leaders from a former church.
- Look for gaps in ministry service.
- Conduct an interview and include the applicant's spouse in the interview. During the interview, secure written permission for a criminal background check and a credit check.
- Ask character questions such as "Have you ever been charged with or convicted of a crime?" and "During your ministry, has your moral life been above reproach?"
- Conduct the criminal background check.

The Southern Baptist Convention, United Methodist church, Roman Catholic Church, and other denominations have put into place extensive and aggressive policies and processes to address sexual misconduct across their network of churches. The Roman Catholic Church should serve as a model for dealing with sexual abuse because it has the most experience dealing with the issue. Mega-churches can learn from Catholic strategies in developing preventive programming. For example, the National Catholic Risk Retention Group, Inc. (National Catholic) created VIRTUS, the brand name that identifies best practices programs designed to help prevent wrongdoing and promote "rightdoing" within religious organizations. According to the program's official website (www.virtus.org), VIRTUS programs constantly and consistently employ several elements as the cornerstone of their methodology. In summary, they are:

- Targeting institutional change and individual behavior modification
- Providing reactive and proactive tools to address those that are exposed to unsafe behavior
- Employing such resources as written materials, web training modules, audiotapes, videotapes, training manuals, and seminars
- Utilizing expert consultants to develop and implement products and services
- Engaging other professional services to develop products and training
- Adhering to best practices, measurable results, and continuous improvements

Best practice is used as a standard. For risk control, it is a standard of effective protocols, procedures, and methods for preventing and responding to risk. The standard requires an organization to demand and enforce "no tolerance" for wrongdoing and open communication channels with employees, volunteers, and others who interact with the organization. When risk is identified, the best practice standard requires the organization to move quickly to eliminate or diminish the risk fairly, effectively, and professionally.

Mega-churches are autonomous but must also design similar policies and processes within their individual churches. Given the number of people who attend and are on their staffs as well as the amount of money these churches take in, developing such programs is easily doable. The consequences of not doing so are multi-million dollar lawsuits and the loss of hundreds or even thousands of current and potential members. After the allegations against Eddie Long became public, the church's donations decreased, it was forced to close its private school, members began leaving, and the church leadership also began leaving (including Reverend Bernice King, the daughter of Dr. Martin Luther King, Jr.). Earl Paulk began the Chapel Hill Harvester Church outside of Atlanta, Georgia, in 1960 with only a few dozen members. In the 1990s, the church has more than 10,000 members and 24 pastors. Paul manipulated a church employee into having an affair with him from 1989 until 2003 by telling her having sex with him was her only path to salvation. He also had an affair with his brother's wife, resulting in an eventual revelation from a paternity test that his adult nephew was actually his son. By 2007, the church's membership had fallen to 1,500. The church's property faced foreclosure in 2009 and was sold to a local church. Paul died the same year.

The plight of mega-churches will be the same as the Roman Catholic Church as such aforementioned scandals continue. As Williams discusses in *America's Religions: From Their Origins to the Twenty-first Century*,

The major event affecting the course of American Catholicism during the early years of the twenty-first century was the national scandal that arose in the late 1990s when the *Boston Globe* began a series of articles reporting that the leadership of the Boston Archdiocese had engaged for many years in the practice of transferring priests accused of sexually abusing children from one parish to another with little attempt at treatment or discipline. Soon similar reports began appearing across the country, with accompanying legal investigations and lawsuits by those claiming to have been victims of clerical abuse. Another response was the/ formation of organizations of laity, such as the Boston-based Voice of the Faithful, determined to seek an accounting from the bishops involved. Some Catholics stopped supporting the Church financially, and others left to join other churches.[6]

Churches regularly build coalitions with local and regional entities. This includes schools, law enforcement officials, social service networks, and private businesses. These coalitions should include relationships that address support to potential, current, and past victims of sexual abuse within the church. Mega-churches should be more open to addressing the proactive and reactive benefits of such coalitions as part of their progressive programs to meet both the spiritual and secular needs of their members. Every church's mission is to teach its members strategies to live healthy lives free of sin. Not reporting the actions of mega-church leaders who commit sexual misconduct violates this mission and makes the church an accomplice in every future act that leader commits.

Preventing and dealing with sexual abuse and misconduct should also be integrated into church programs. Although it may be an uncomfortable topic, it can be integrated into or presented as the main topic of seminars and workshops. There should even be sessions where children are taught how to behave when approached by strangers, how to recognize if someone is acting inappropriately toward them, and how to report incidents to parents and church officials. The church should hold seminars for parents, family, friends, and coworkers about how to look for signs their family members and acquaintances are being sexually abused. This is especially in cases involving children. Most people do not know how to recognize when a child, family member, or friend is being abused. Early warning signs are often mistaken for mood swings or side effects of working too hard. Resources and information from the National Center for Victims of Crime (www.victimsofcrime.org) provides just one example of the types of information churches should integrate into their programs:

Many sexually abused children exhibit physical, behavioral and emotional symptoms. Some physical signs are pain or irritation to the genital area, vaginal or penile discharge and difficulty with urination. Victims of known assailants may experience less physical trauma because such injuries might attract suspicion. Behavioral changes often precede physical symptoms as the first indicators of sexual abuse. Behavioral signs include nervous or aggressive behavior toward adults, sexual provocativeness before an appropriate age and the use of alcohol and other drugs. Boys are more likely than girls to act out in aggressive and antisocial ways as a result of abuse. Children may say such things as, "My mother's boyfriend does things to me when she's not there," or "I'm afraid to go home tonight."[7]

Notice that this information speaks directly to the issue in blunt terms. This type of presentation may be difficult for a church to embrace. However, dealing with sex abuse requires frank discussions that clearly outline issues and appropriate actions to deal with those issues. Using soft jargon or speaking on a high level will not suffice. If a minister's sermon can address sodomy and adultery in a hell-and-brimstone tone, certainly a church should be willing to have an open discussion about the physical and mental effects of sex abuse on a child.

Again, the reporting process for both adults and children should be private and free from attribution. Any reported incidents should be immediately investigated. In the case of children, law enforcement officials should be involved. Counselors outside of the church should also be used to provide victims with unbiased support. The church should assume all expenses for victims' counseling and legal support.

Churches must also implement radical ideas to prevent and deal with sexual misconduct. They should establish call centers for anonymous tips related to wrongdoing. Mega-churches have hundreds of volunteers, so they have the resources to establish such centers. For victims of current and past sexual abuse, churches should also establish support networks that are open to members and those in the community. This fosters a community service that is vitally needed, particularly in geographic areas where such services either do not exist or are overwhelmed with demand. Since mega-churches are predominantly based in and around urban centers, they undoubtedly have ample demand for such services. They should offer families and their communities outreach services through which victims can receive counseling services outside of the church. This reduces the stigma and shame of having to report to an office where they may feel what has happened to them will be publicly revealed. Churches should collaborate with schools, women's shelters, and centers for abuse victims to provide support and receive collaborative assistance.

Of course, church leaders' personal accountability is the primary way to stop acts of sexual misconduct. This is especially true since many past incidents have occurred outside of the church with prostitutes, mistresses, or people met on the Internet. As detailed throughout the book, some victims have not even known the culprit was a minister. Taking responsibility and accountability for the faith and service these leaders have dedicated themselves is not only expected but required. Jim Swilley is an example of a minister who did just this. He was the founder and pastor of Church in the Now in Conyers, Georgia. In 2010, he revealed to his congregation that he is gay. Swilley was married to a woman and the father of four children. He struggled with being gay for most of his life, and his wife Debye knew he was gay when they got married. She supported his decision to go public. Swilley decided to reveal his sexuality because of a recent surge in bullying of and suicides by gay teens, even though he knew the announcement could end his career. He received a great amount of support from within and outside of the church to the point that his Facebook page reached the maximum number of allowable friends.[8] His courage may have saved hundreds of lives. His confession came with no prompting by a scandal or public exposure of wrongdoing.

In *Moral Ambition: Mobilization and Social Outreach in Evangelical Megachurches*, Elisha describes the need for accountability in mega-churches through delegating responsibilities to others in the church:

Accountability functions among evangelicals as a theological and instructional paradigm that is applicable to every aspect of their lives, from how they run their homes and businesses to matters of sexual morality and family life to even broader notions of religious, civic, and political responsibility.... As an organizational principle, the concept of accountability helps to legitimize the authority of church pastors and elders, especially in mega-churches with large budgets and influence. By delegating pastoral and administrative responsibilities among teams made up of clergy, staff, and lay volunteers, mega-churches maintain bureaucratic efficiency and also provide visible structures of corporate accountability, which is desirable in light of high-profile corruption and sex scandals involving celebrity pastors and wealthy televangelists, which never fail to draw negative public attention and media scrutiny.[9]

It cannot be stated enough that when a minister is accused of wrongdoing, the church must take immediate action. Just as schools and police departments do, the church should immediately suspend the minister (even if with pay) until a thorough investigation of the alleged wrongdoing can be completed if the allegations presented are initially believed to be credible. If there are suspicions about the allegations, the minister can be allowed to actively remain in office but should be clearly told what adverse actions will be taken if the allegations are true. During the investigation, the minister should not be allowed to complicate the investigation by having private meetings with the accuser, the accuser's family, or collaborating witnesses. In addition, he should not be allowed to attempt to sway the church membership by making the incident being investigated a part of a sermon or speech. As stated earlier, if the allegations involve illegal activities such as prostitution, rape, or child molestation, the church must gain assistance from law enforcement officials and/or social service experts.

Additionally, care must be taken to ensure the church leader is aware of his rights, for example, seeking legal counsel and being advised of the full nature of the accusations. If the church leader is formally charged, the church should assume all expenses related to legally supporting the victim(s). If the minister is found guilty, he should be removed from the church, or his duties should be greatly altered if he is allowed to remain. For example, he may not be allowed to have any direct contact with children, to have private counseling sessions, or to conduct baptisms if any of these duties are similar to the circumstance of the act of sexual misconduct. A minister allowed to remain should submit to close monitoring and personal counseling from a source outside the church. Counseling should also be provided to the minister's spouse and other close family members.

As discussed in previous chapters, mega-church ministers sometimes commit acts of wrongdoing due in part to the nature of their jobs. They are in highly stressful occupations. This stress leads some to engage in sex, alcohol, or other negative behaviors. There are several coping mechanisms they should adopt. Just as mega-church leaders need to have full-time attorneys, they must also have counseling services readily available. A confidential counselor for the minister should be permanent and even part of the church staff. The individual in this role should hold recurring meetings with the minister, and even his spouse together and separately, to discuss whatever issues are causing him concern, challenges he is facing, and any personal issues he is dealing with. This includes any thoughts or compulsions that would negatively impact the church. Ministers should have required annual vacations, paid sabbaticals when needed, and paid sick leave. To ensure they are leading mentally and physically healthy lives, they should be given the same job-related benefits as public and private leaders.

Chapter 7

Conclusion: The Future of Mega-Churches in a Climate of Sexual Corruption

There is much debate over whether mega-churches will continue to exist and, if they do, their future level of influence on religion in the United States. The phenomenon of mega-churches occurred rapidly in the context of historical religion. They were established as a result of a social and cultural shift in attitudes by the general population during the 1970s. A general distrust of government and organized institutions such as the Roman Catholic and Episcopalian churches, coupled with a growth in spirituality, led to the popularity of mega-churches because they were autonomous entities that catered to both the spiritual and secular needs of their members. However, the popularity of mega-churches is likely to wane as the generation that gave rise to their popularity grows older and shifts occur in the societal and cultural thinking. As Skye Jethani states in the article "Mega-Churches: When Will the Bubble Burst?," "The cultural and demographic conditions that have fueled much of the mega-church movement, multiplication and growth are changing. And whenever a new movement tries to leap from one generation to the next there are some who don't clear the gap."[1] For example, as the U.S. population becomes increasingly urban and more influenced by other cultures (particularly Hispanic and Asian), and as the concept of family changes (e.g., a growing number of interracial marriages and same-sex parents), it remains to be seen what role Protestant religion and large religious entities will play.

The future of mega-churches will be heavily dependent upon how they are perceived by the general population. Because they serve such large congregations and are heavily involved in their local communities, scandals and perceptions of wrongdoing by their leaders will be detrimental to their attracting new members, retaining the ones they already have, and receiving financial support. These scandals and perceptions of wrongdoing will even impact whether federal, state, and local governments develop new policies regulating church operations. Acts of sexual misconduct by church leaders have perhaps the most damaging impact on people's perception of a church, given that mega-church leaders are pillars of their churches. These acts give lead others to feel that the minister really has no real concern for the church other than how much money it makes, nor does he have the devout faith required to lead others religiously. These acts also lead to the perception that fallen leaders would do further wrong such as embezzling money or manipulating church members for personal gain. The worst cases are sexual abuse of minors. Such actions are not only against the law, but they are also deemed offensive by potentially every segment of society. They draw the greatest distain from communities and lead to quick intervention into church affairs from external entities.

Unlike traditional and formal religious organizations such as the Roman Catholic Church, mega-churches do not have a foundation based upon centuries of institutionalized religion. Mega-churches are predominantly homogenous entities. A major scandal in the Roman Catholic Church is handled within a hierarchical system that is able to shield the church from a certain level of scrutiny, persecution, and prosecution. The negative acts of one person or several cannot permanently damage the image of the entire institution. This is mainly because the Church's existence is based upon its religious tradition rather than the charisma of a single person. A single sex scandal in a mega-church can permanently damage its image, even if a new leader takes over. In extreme cases, such scandal can cause a church to close.

As stated earlier in this chapter, another implication of sexual scandals in mega-churches is close scrutiny or possibly federal and state legislation restricting the religious freedom of churches. States are already debating loosening the statute of limitations for crimes related to sexual abuse. Currently, states set legal deadlines as to when a victim can bring suits against ministers, teachers, youth counselors, and family members. There are time limitations for prosecutors to press charges. However, the growing number of sex abuse incidents in churches, schools, and other entities has prompted some states to consider lengthening the limits or doing away with them all together. This would substantially increase the financial and legal liabilities for individuals who commit sex abuse and organizations that do not take proactive and reactive steps to adequately deal with incidents. It remains to be seen what other state and federal actions will be taken that may legally diminish the line between religious autonomy and state intervention.

In addition to sex-related scandals, mega-churches are facing challenges that threaten their futures. These challenges include aging memberships, aging leaders without clear succession plans, changing demographics that are placing whites in the minority (whites are the majority of mega-church members), and less commitment by young people to spending Sundays in church versus engaging in sports or other recreational activities. Although 30 percent of mega-church members are between the ages of 25 and 44, the majority (65%) are 45 and over.[2] Over the next few decades, the survival of mega-churches will rest in the hands of Generations X and Y. Unlike Baby Boomers, a large percentage of both younger generations do not support organized religion or are not religious at all. They lend greater support to issues not supported by older generations such as same-sex marriage, interracial marriage, abortion, and immigration.

Recent research shows younger Americans are dramatically less likely to attend church or participate in any form of organized religion than their parents or grandparents. While the average proportion of the general population with no religious affiliation has historically remained between 5 and 10 percent, the rate for young Americans has reached 30 to 40 percent. This latter category includes those in both Generation X and Generation Y. A primary reason for this lack of religion is the view by youth that the doctrines of organized religions are intolerant and rigid. The negative consequences of the findings of this research include lower social and civic involvement by youth than older generations, and a lower tendency to vote, volunteer, and give to charities.[3]

In *The Emerging Church: Vintage Christianity for New Generations*, Kimball and Warren analyzed youth church attendance. They show a decline in religion among young people. They quote the following statistical data from researcher George Barna:[4]

- Out of all age groups, those 18 to 32 are the least likely to describe themselves as religious, as Christian, or as committed Christians.
- Young adults today in the U.S. seem the most open to exploring faiths other than Christianity.
- Young adults are avoiding church; Church attendance is declining by generation.

- Compared with teens throughout the past twenty years, today's teenagers have the lowest likelihood of attending church when they are living independent of their parents.
- The data regarding young adults also post the possibility that churches are losing ground in terms of influence and may need to consider new approaches.

It remains to be seen how this shift in religious support by young people will impact mega-churches. The nondenominational affiliation of mega-churches may attract more youth, as well as teachings and sermons that focus on modern issues rather than scripture. At the same time, young people will be attracted by mega-churches' modern music, social activities, and culturally driven programs rather than traditional ceremonies. However, the rigid and sometimes bigoted teachings of their ministers may then push these young people away. Rainer and Rainer found this to be the case among teenagers. In *Essential Church?: Reclaiming a Generation of Dropouts*, they reported that

the most glaring issue of estrangement for eighteen to twenty-two-year-olds is the interminable gap between their personal beliefs and their church's stated beliefs. In other words, the church's stated external beliefs, covenant, or confession goes against the personal and internal belief structure of these younger adults. Only 53 percent of all young adult churchgoers state that they are in line with the beliefs of their church. The dropout crisis isn't found in the style, venue, or programs, or locations of the church. This crisis is much deeper; it runs to the core of the doctrinal truths of the church. Only half of our young adults agree with the church's teachings.[5]

Church leaders themselves are part of the Baby Boomer generation. Their average age is 50, and most will be retiring in the next 10 to 15 years. Because most founded, lead, and control their churches, most have no clear succession plan in place. Some will pass the baton of leadership from father to son. Other churches will wait to make replacement plans until their church leader announces retirement or leaves. However, there is a growing shortage of ministers. Some describe the situation as critical. Ministers of all denominations are leaving the church in large numbers. Fewer young people are entering the profession due to their declining faith but also because of their perceptions of what life as a minister would mean. They do not believe their lives would be full in terms of social and cultural fulfillment, nor that they would be able to lead full family lives. Beyond believing their lives would be rigid, they also see a life in religion as they do a life in politics. Ministers are often scrutinized and sometimes demonized as politicians are when they make mistakes such as having affairs, being drunk in public, or being accused of stealing money. They become the target of media attention and can be shunned by the public.

The succession of mega-church leaders is a rocky process, especially under circumstances when the church leader was involved in sexual misconduct. Many churches lose most of their members or close entirely. Even when sexual misconduct has not occurred, it is a difficult process given that the church's popularity and success was due to the charisma and leadership of a single person. The name and image of the church are completely intertwined with the identity of its leader. Thinking about the continuation of the church without its current leader is an unpleasant task for church members, staff, and other leaders. There are the issues of trust related to whoever replaces the current leader, the appropriate retirement plan for the current leader, and how the leader's family should be cared for by the church if the leader dies. For these reasons, successions are often chaotic.

The events surrounding the succession of new leadership in the Crystal Cathedral in Garden Grove, California, is an example. The church and its international program *Hour of Power* was founded by Robert H. Schuller as the Garden Grove Community Church in 1955. The original church was opened in a drive-in movie theater. Services were eventually moved to the magnificent Crystal Cathedral, which was dedicated on September 14, 1980. At the height of the church's success, the *Hour of Power* was the most widely watched hour-long church service in the world, and the local church had 10,000 members. Schuller announced his retirement in 2006, and his son assumed the role of senior pastor. The elder Schuller removed his son from the position in 2008 due to what he described as "lack of a shared vision." The son publicly stated the church split was due to sibling rivalry over church leadership. Schuller's daughter was then appointed the church's leader in 2010. In that same year, the church announced it was bankrupt. In 2012, Schuller's daughter announced she was leaving the church to start her own. Later that year, the Crystal Cathedral was purchased by the Roman Catholic Dioceses of Orange, California, for $57.7 million and renamed Christ Cathedral.[6]

When the church's leader leaves, mega-churches often face one of two futures: extreme decline or extreme growth. In the former case, they decline as the generation that caused their growth disappears. Davis provides the opinion of many in *More Than a Purpose: An Evangelical Response to Rick Warren and the Megachurch Movement*:

The warehouse approach to religion does not attract the younger crowd. They cherish smaller, more informal, more intimate forms of Christianity. The megachurch will pass away as boomers age, just as mainline churches have declined with the aging of the World War II generation. Even though mega-churches try to be all things to all people, they have a negative image among the newest generation of Christians. To believers in their twenties, mega-churches are large, impersonal, corporate entities. They are seen as the product of an older generation that shops at Wal-Mart and thinks Disney World is a dream vacation. Just as liberal Protestant churches have declined in both attendance and influence, so the mega-church movement will also pass slowly into irrelevance in future decades.[7]

In the latter case, growth occurs through the continued growth of some churches, the merger of others, and the establishment of new mega-churches formed to address new social and cultural shifts. If mega-churches evolve into having memberships or hundreds of thousands and sermons in stadiums, will a single leader be able to adequately lead them? Will there be any personal accountability as churches increase their use of technology to reach members who are more nationally and globally dispersed? For example, one prediction of the future of mega-churches is that they will have to rely on multisite locations in order to maintain their membership levels. One factor that has allowed mega-church leaders who have committed sexual misconduct to do so has been their freedom in traveling. Greater travel requirements, increased stress in meeting the needs of dispersed members, and greater demands in maintaining membership levels are all potentially causative factors in leading mega-church ministers to engage in questionable behaviors.

Another question for the future of mega-churches is just how secular they will become in their worship styles and ideology. Those of today have already abandoned formalized religious practices, basing their sermons strictly on the Bible and having worship services based on traditional church services. To attract young people who are already less religious, will mega-churches abandon even more of any semblance of religion in their services? If so, how will this impact what behavior church leaders deem acceptable and unacceptable?

Beyond developing strategies to ensure their church leaders stay out of trouble, in order to remain socially viable, mega-churches will also have to adapt how they meet the needs of their members and the community. Most have already begun taking some steps to do this. Mega-churches are becoming more involved in not only their local communities, but also national and international causes. They provide help during natural disasters as well as support the homeless, single mothers, and children needing all kinds of social, family, and educational assistance. They also network with other mega-churches as well as smaller churches. Some share human and financial resources with smaller churches in order to spread their message and serve a larger congregation. Others foster networks that allow both their members and members of other churches to join.

Mega-churches also serve their members by taking the church's message to its members. They are constructing satellite campus, as discussed throughout the book, but also holding programs in community centers, schools, stadiums, and other locations outside the central church. Still, all of this will be overshadowed by a church leader committing sex abuse and other acts of sexual misconduct.

Appendix

Top 10 Mega-Churches in America

1. Lakewood Church: Texas; Pastor, Joel Osteen; Members, 47,000
2. Willow Creek Community Church: Illinois; Pastor, Bill Hybels; Members, 23,500
3. Second Baptist Church: Texas; Pastor, Ed Young; Members, 24,000
4. Saddleback Church: California; Pastor, Rick Warren; Members, 22,000
5. Life Church: Oklahoma; Pastor, Craig Groeschel; Members, 19,900
6. Southeast Christian Church: Kentucky; Pastor, Dave Stone; Members, 18,000
7. North Point Community Church: Georgia; Pastor, Andy Stanley; Members, 17,700
8. Thomas Road Baptist Church: Virginia; Pastor, Jonathan Falwell; Members, 17,445
9. Calvary Chapel: California; Pastor, Robert Coy; Members, 17,000
10. The Potter's House: Texas; Pastor, T. D. Jakes; Members, 17,000

Source: Mark Nickens, "Megachurches," *Summaries of Christianity*, Christiantimelines. com. Copyright © 2009.

Notes

CHAPTER 1

1. Erling Jorstad, *Popular Religion in America: The Evangelical Voice.* Contributions to the Study of Religion (Westport, CT: Greenwood Press, 1993), p. 195.

2. Scott Thumma, Dave Travis, and Warren Bird, *Mega-Churches Today 2005.* Retrieved from http://hirr.hartsem.edu/org/faith_mega-churches_research.html#research on September 15, 2011.

3. Anne C. Loveland and Otis B. Wheeler, *From Meetinghouse to Megachurch: A Material and Cultural History* (Columbia, MO: University of Missouri Press, 2003), p. 14.

4. Ross Douthat, *Bad Religion: How We Became a Nation of Heretics* (New York: Free Press, 2012), p. 62.

5. Stephen Ellingson, *The Megachurch and the Mainline: Remaking Religious Tradition in the Twenty-First Century* (Chicago: The University of Chicago Press, 2007), p. 10.

6. Bryan S. Turner (ed.), *The New Blackwell Companion to the Sociology of Religion* (Malden, MA: Blackwell Publishing, 2010), p. 259.

7. Gilbert Bilrzikian and John Ortberg, *Community 101: Reclaiming the Local Church as Community of Oneness* (Grand Rapids, MI: Zondervan Publishing House, 1997), p. 48.

8. Loveland and Wheeler, *From Meetinghouse to Megachurch*, p. 5.

9. A. Kohut and B. Stokes, *America against the World* (New York: Henry Holt and Company, 2006), p. 103.

10. Thomas White and John M. Yeats, *Franchising McChurch: Feeding Our Obsession with Easy Christianity* (Colorado Springs, Colorado: David C. Cook, 2009), p. 137.

11. Evans-Cowley, Jennifer S. "Good Heavens! Texas Churches Grow to Biblical Proportions." *Commercial Markets*, April 2007. Retrieved from http://recenter.tamu.edu/pdf/1809.pdf on July 4, 2012.

12. John Dart, "The Trend toward Bigger Churches: Going Mega," *Christian Century* (July 27, 2010): 22.

13. James B. Twitchell, *Shopping for God: How Christianity Went from In Your Heart to In Your Face* (New York: Simon & Schuster, 2007), p. 3.

14. Ibid., p. 68.

15. Peter W. Williams, *America's Religion: From Their Origins to the Twenty-first Century* (Chicago: University of Illinois Press, 2008), p. 390.

16. Robert D. Putnam and Lewis Feldstein, *Better Together: Restoring the American Community* (New York: Simon & Schuster, 2003), p. 127.

17. Jesse Bogan, "American's Biggest Mega-Churches," *Forbes* (June 26, 2009). Retrieved from http://www.forbes.com/2009/06/26/americas-biggest-mega-churches-business-mega-churches.html on June 23, 2012.

18. Colleen Pepper, *Inside the World of Executive Pastors: Leadership Network's 2009 Survey* (Leadership Network, 2009), p. 1. Retrieved from www.leadnet.org on December 14, 2011.

19. Ibid., p. 5.

20. Ibid., p. 6.

21. Ibid., p. 9.

22. Scott Thumma and Dave Travis, *Beyond Megachurch Myths: What We Can Learn from America's Largest Churches* (San Francisco: John Wiley & Sons, 2007).

23. Bogan, 2009.

24. Lyle E. Schaller, *The Seven-Day-a-Week Church* (Nashville: Abingdon, 1992), p. 144.

25. Bruce L. Shelley, *Church History in Plain Language* (3rd ed.) (Nashville: Thomas Nelson, 2008), p. 479.

26. Association of Religion Data Archives (ARDA). *United Methodist Church*, 2012. Retrieved from http://www.thearda.com/Denoms/D_1469.asp on July 3, 2012.

27. Pew Forum on Religion and Public Life. *U.S. Religious Landscape Survey (Religious Affiliation: Diverse and Dynamic)* (Washington, D.C.: Pew Research Center, February 2008), p. 5.

CHAPTER 2

1. Mara Einstein, *Brands of Faith: Marketing Religion in a Commercial Age* (New York: Routledge, 2008), p. xi.

2. Skye Jethani, "Mega-Churches: When Will the Bubble Burst?" *Huffington Post*, November 8, 2011. Retrieved from http://www.huffingtonpost.com on December 15, 2011.

3. Box Office Mojo. *Jumping the Broom*. Retrieved from http://www.boxofficemojo.com/movies/?id=jumpingthebroom.htm on October 1, 2012.

4. Scott Thumma and Dave Travis, *Beyond Megachurch Myths: What We Can Learn from America's Largest Churches* (San Francisco: John Wiley & Sons, 2007), p. 60.

5. Warren Bird, *Megachurches as Spectator Religion: Using Social Network Theory and Free-rider Theory to Understand the Spiritual Vitality of America's Largest-Attendance Churches* (New York: Fordham University, 2007), p. 127.

6. William C. Symonds, Brian Grow, and John Cady, "Earthly Empires," *Businessweek*, (May 23, 2005). Retrieved from http://www.businessweek.com/stories/2005-05-22/earthly-empires on August 5, 2012.

7. Stanley J. Grenz and Roy D. Bell, *Betrayal of Trust: Confronting and Preventing Clergy Sexual Misconduct* (Grand Rapids, MI: Baker Books, 2001), p. 18.

8. Mark Laaser and Nancy Myer Hopkins, *Restoring the Soul of a Church: Healing Congregations Wounded by Clergy Sexual Misconduct* (Collegeville, MN: Order of St. Benedict, 1995), pp. 42–49.

9. Nils Friberg and Mark R. Laaser, *Before the Fall: Preventing Pastoral Sexual Abuse* (Collegeville, MN: Order of St. Benedict, 1998), p. 18.

10. Mark Laaser, *Healing the Wounds of Sexual Addiction* (Grand Rapids, MI: Zondervan, 2004), p. 43.

11. Max Weber, *Essays in Sociology* (New York: Oxford University Press, 1946), p. 80.

12. Ricky W. Griffin, *Management* (2nd ed.) (Boston: Houghton Mifflin Company, 1987) pp. 421–423.

13. Weber, *Essays*, p. 212.

14. Joris Lammers, Diederik A. Stapel, and Adam D. Galinsky, "Power Increases Hypocrisy: Moralizing in Reasoning, Immorality in Behavior," *Psychological Science* 21 (2010): 737–744.

15. Luiza Oleszczuk, "Bishop Joseph Walker III Accused of Sexual Assault by 4 Women." *The Christian Post*, March 1, 2012. Retrieved from http://www.christianpost.com/news/bishop-joseph-walker-iii-accused-of-sexual-assault-by-4-women-70631/ on August 1, 2012.

16. Sam Hodges, "Exclusive: Former employee sues Daystar founder Marcus Lamb over his extramarital affair with another employee." *Dallasnews.com*, December 3, 2010. Retrieved from www.dallasnews.com on June 23, 2012.

17. Dana Rasmussen, *Behind Bars in America, Vol. 3: Federal Prisons in North and South Carolina and Inmates Like Bernie Madoff, Jim Bakker, Mark Whitacre, and More* (United States: Webster's Digital Services, 2011), p. 84.

18. Jim Spellman, "New Haggard accuser: 'He really thought he was invincible'." *CNN.com*, January 29 2009. Retrieved from http://edition.cnn.com/2009/CRIME/01/28/colorado.church.haggard/index.html on October 14, 2012.

19. *Atlanta Journal-Constitution*, "2005 AJC report: Bishop Eddie Long Benefits from His Own Church's Charity: Between 1997 and 2000, Eddie Long Received $3.07 Million in Compensation" (August 28, 2005). Retrieved from www.ajc.com on October 14, 2011.

138 Notes

20. Candace R. Benyei, *Understanding Clergy Misconduct in Religious Systems: Scapegoating, Family Secrets, and the Abuse of Power* (Binghamton, NY: Haworth Pastoral Press, 1998), p. 74.

21. Mary Gail Frawley-O'Dea, *Perversion of Power: Sexual Abuse in the Catholic Church* (Nashville: Vanderbilt University Press, 2007), p. 21.

22. Karen A. McClintock, *Preventing Sexual Abuse in Congregations: A Resource for Leaders* (Herndon, VA: Alban Institute, 2004), p. 78.

23. *AllPsych Online*, Retrieved from http://allpsych.com (2012).

24. Ibid.

25. Laaser, *Healing the Wounds*, p. 43.

26. Grenz and Bell, *Betrayal of Trust*, p. 41.

27. Kathleen A. Brehony, *Awakening at Midlife* (New York: Riverhead Books, 1996), p. 2.

28. Carl G. Jung, *Modern Man in Search of a Soul* (New York: Harvest Books, 1933).

29. David B. Wexler, *When Good Men Behave Badly: Change Your Behavior, Change Your Relationship* (Oakland, CA: New Harbinger Publications, 2004), p. 70.

30. Dave Early, *Pastoral Leadership is . . . How to Shepherd God's People with Passion and Confidence* (Nashville, Tennessee: B&H Publishing Group, 2012), p. 7.

31. John A. Sanford, *Ministry Burnout* (Louisville, KY, Westminster/John Knox Press, 1982), pp. 5–18.

32. William N. Grosch and David C. Olsen, "Clergy Burnout: An Integrative Approach," *Journal of Clinical Psychology* 56, no. 5 (2000): 619–632.

33. *National Institute of Justice Journal*. "On-the-Job Stress in Policing: Reducing It, Preventing It" (January 2000), p. 20.

34. Patrick J. Carnes, *Out of the Shadows: Understanding Sexual Addiction* (Center City, MN: Hazelden, 2001), p. 74.

35. Laaser, *Healing the Wounds*, p. 27.

36. Lammers et al., "Power Increases Hypocrisy," p. 743.

37. Brentin Mock, "Bishop Eddie Long." *Intelligence Report* 125 (Spring 2007). Retrieved from http://www.splcenter.org/get-informed/intelligence-report/browse-all-issues/2007/spring/face-right/bishop-eddie-long on July 5, 2012.

38. Ibid.

39. Alex Murashko, "Sex Addiction: Are Pastors More Vulnerable to Sexual Temptation?" *Christian Post* (June 25, 2012). Retrieved from http://www.christianpost.com/news/sex-addiction-are-pastors-more-vulnerable-to-sexual-temptation-67935/ on April 2, 2012.

40. Elizabeth A. Horst, *Questions and Answers about Clergy Misconduct* (Collegeville, MN: Order of St. Benedict, 2000), p. 16.

41. Ibid., p. 17.

42. Omri Elisha, *Moral Ambition: Mobilization and Social Outreach in Evangelical Megachurches (The Anthropology of Christianity)* (Los Angeles: University of California Press, 2011), p. 171.

43. Don Boys, "Mess in Memphis: Bellevue Baptist, Another Mega-Church in Trouble!" (May 14, 2007). Retrieved from www.CSTNews.com on June 13, 2012.

44. Ben Witherington, *Looking Haggard, Ted Steps Aside*. November 3, 2006. Retrieved from http://benwitherington.blogspot.com/2006/11/looking- haggard-ted-steps-aside.html on July 3, 2012.

45. Gary Neuman, *The Truth about Cheating: Why Men Stray and What You Can Do to Prevent It* (Hoboken, NJ: Wiley & Sons, 2008), p. 17.

46. Center for Ministerial Care, *Ministerial Marriage and Family* (Cleveland, TN, 1998), p. 3.

CHAPTER 3

1. National Center for Victims of Crime, *Child Sex Abuse, 2012*. Retrieved from http://www.ncvc.org/ncvc/main.aspx?dbName=DocumentViewer&DocumentID=32315#9 on June 21, 2012.

2. Mark Chaves and Diana Garland, "The Prevalence of Clergy Sexual Advances toward Adults in Their Congregations," *Journal for the Scientific Study of Religion* 48, no. 4 (2009): 817–824.

3. RAINN (2012). Retrieved from http://www.rainn.org/statistics/.

4. Shapiro, 2007.

5. NCTSN.org (2012).

6. David Finkelhor, "Today, Sex Abuse Victims Are Less Alone," *CNN* (June 20, 2012). Retrieved from http://www.cnn.com/2012/06/20/opinion/finkelhor-sandusky-child-abuse/index.html?hpt=hp_bn7 on July 15, 2012.

7. Randall Easton Wickham and Janet West, *Therapeutic Work with Sexually Abused Children* (Thousand Oaks, CA: Sage Publications, Ltd., 2002), p. 4.

8. RAINN.

9. Graham Martin, Helen A. Bergen, Angela S. Richardson, Leigh Roeger, and Stephen Allison, "Sexual Abuse and Suicidality: Gender Differences in a Large Community Sample of Adolescents," *Child Abuse & Neglect* 28 (2004): 495–496.

10. Susan Wise Bauer, *The Art of Public Grovel: Sexual Sin and Public Confession in America* (Princeton, NJ: Princeton University Press, 2008), pp. 237–238.

11. Alison Clarke-Stewart and Cornelia Brentano, *Divorce: Causes and Consequences (Current Perspectives in Psychology)* (New Haven, CT: Yale University Press, 2006).

CHAPTER 4

1. Scott Thumma, *Exploring the Megachurch Phenomena: Their Characteristics and Cultural Context*, Hartford Institute for Religion Research (2011). Retrieved from http://hirr.hartsem.edu/bookshelf/thumma_article2.html on December 11, 2011.

2. Internal Revenue Service (IRS), *Tax Guide for Religious Organizations: Benefits and Responsibilities under the Federal Tax Law* (Washington, D.C.: Internal Revenue Service, 2012), p. 3.

3. Associated Press, *Secret Service, IRS Investigate Atlanta Megachurch*, FoxNews.com (October 21, 2011). Retrieved from http://www.foxnews.com/us/2011/10/21/secret-service-irs-investigate-atlanta-megachurch/ on November 2, 2011.

4. Donald H. Matthews, *Sexual Abuse of Power in the Black Church: Sexual Misconduct in the African American Churches* (Bloomington, IN: WestBow Press, 2012), pp. 3–4.

5. Susan Finch. "DA says music minister exposed teen to HIV." *The New Orleans Times-Picayune*, August 11, 2000.

6. Elizabeth A. Horst, *Questions and Answers about Clergy Misconduct* (Collegeville, MN: Order of St. Benedict, 2000), p. 21.

7. Candace R. Benyei, *Understanding Clergy Misconduct in Religious Systems: Scapegoating, Family Secrets, and the Abuse of Power* (Binghamton, NY: Haworth Pastoral Press, 1998), p. 103.

8. Art Moore, "Mega-Church Pastor Resigns, but Denies Sexual Misdeeds," *Christianity Today* 12, no. 8 (July 13, 1998): 26.

9. Irving L. Janis, and Leon Mann, *Decision Making* (New York: Free Press, 1977); Michael R. Callaway and James K. Esser, "Groupthink: Effects of Cohesiveness and Problem-Solving Procedures on Group Decision Making," *Social Behavior and Personality* 12, no. 2 (1984): 157–164.

10. Irving L. Janis, *Victims of Groupthink* (New York: Houghton Mifflin, 1972); Janis, *Groupthink: Psychological Studies of Policy Decisions and Fiascoes* (2nd ed.) (New York: Houghton Mifflin, 1982).

11. John L. Mastrogiovanni, *Why Ministers Fall: In Search of the Holy Grail* (Seattle: CreateSpace, 2009), p. 14.

12. Stoyan Zaimov, "Pastor Darrell Gilyard's Sex Offender Status Divides Fla. Community." *The Christian Post*, February 23, 2012. Retrieved from http://www.christianpost.com/news/pastors-sex-offender-status-divides-fla-community-70039/ on July 25, 2012.

13. Karen A. McClintock, *Preventing Sexual Abuse in Congregations: A Resource for Leaders* (Herndon, VA: Alban Institute, 2004), pp. 4–5.

14. Katherine T. Phan, "Bernice King Leaving Eddie Long's Megachurch to Start New Ministry."*The Christian Post*, May 31, 2011. Retrieved from http://www.christianpost.com/news/bernice-king-leaving-eddie-longs-church-to-launch-new-ministry-50707/ on August 3, 2012.

15. Donald B. Cozzens, *The Changing Face of the Priesthood: A Reflection on the Priest's Crisis of Soul* (Collegeville, MN: Liturgical Press, 2000), p. 125.

16. Bishop Accountability. *Sexual Abuse by U.S. Catholic Clergy: Settlements and Monetary Awards in Civil Suits*. Retrieved from http://www.bishop-accountability.org/settlements/ on October 15, 2012.

17. James Eng, "Jehovah's Witnesses Ordered to Pay More Than $20 Million to Woman Who Said She Was Sexually Abused," NBC News (June 15, 2012). Retrieved from http://usnews.msnbc.msn.com on June 30, 2012.

18. Gustav Niebuhr, "Mormons Paying $3 Million to Settle Sex Abuse Case." The *New York Times*, September 5, 2001. Retrieved from http://www.nytimes.com/2001/09/05/us/mormons-paying-3-million-to-settle-sex-abuse-case.html on October 15, 2012.

19. Paul McKay, "Mormons Caught Up in Wave of Pedophile Accusations/Church Deals with Abuse Cases without Reporting Them, Critics Say," *Houston Chronicle* (May 9, 1999), p. 1A.

20. Associated Press, "Data Shed Light on Child Sexual Abuse by Protestant Clergy," *New York Times* (June 16, 2007), p. A11.

21. Mental Health America. *Co-dependency*. Alexandria, Virginia: Mental Health America, 2012. Retrieved from http://www.mentalhealthamerica.net/go/codependency on July 6, 2012.

CHAPTER 5

1. Lydia Saad, "U.S. Confidence in Organized Religion at Low Point," *Gallup Politics* (July 12, 2012). Retrieved from www.gallup.com on August 2, 2012.

2. Scott Thumma and Warren Bird, *Not Who You Think They Are: The Real Story of People Who Attend America's Megachurches* (Hartford, CT: Hartford Institute for Religious Research, 2009), p. 2.

3. Ross Douthat, *Bad Religion: How We Became a Nation of Heretics* (New York: Free Press, 2012), p. 4.

4. Kumar, 2012.

5. Roger Oakland, *Faith Undone: The Emerging Church: A New Reformation or an End-Time Deception* (Silverton, OR: Lighthouse Trails Publishing, 2007), p. 29.

6. Helguero, 2005.

7. *Bloomberg Businessweek*, "Earthly Empires: How Evangelical Churches Are Booming from the Business Playbook" (May 23, 2005). Retrieved from http://www.businessweek.com/magazine/content/05_21/b3934001_mz001.htm on June 25, 2012.

8. Robbie B. H. Goh, "Hillsong and 'Mega-Church' Practice: Semiotics, Spatial Logic and the Embodiment of Contemporary Evangelical Protestantism," *Material Religion* 4, no. 3 (November 2008): 288.

9. Lyle E. Schaller, "Mega-Church!" *Christianity Today* 34, no. 4 (March 5, 1990): 21–22.

10. Kathy Lohr, "Senator Probes Mega-Churches' Finances," *NPR* (December 4, 2007). Retrieved from www.npr.org on January 3, 2012.

11. Barry A. Kosmin and Ariela Keysar, *American Religious Identification Survey (ARIS 2008)* (Hartford, CT: Trinity College, 2009).

12. Thomas Dixon, *Science and Religion: A Very Short Introduction* (New York: Oxford University Press, 2008), pp. 114–115.

13. Stephen Hunt, *Religion and Everyday Life* (New York: Routledge, 2005), pp. 62–63.

14. Julian Baggini, *Atheism: A Very Short Introduction* (New York: Oxford University Press, 2003), p. 37.

15. Ibid., p. 38.

16. Rachel Elizabeth Dew, Stephanie S. Daniel, Tonya D. Armstrong, David B. Goldston, Mary Frances Triplett, and Harold G. Koenig, "Religion/Spirituality and Adolescent Psychiatric Symptoms: A Review," *Child Psychiatry & Human Development* 39 (December 1, 2008): 381–398.

17. Mark Chaves, *American Religion: Contemporary Trends* (Princeton, NJ: Princeton University Press, 2011).

CHAPTER 6

1. Joe Dallas and Nancy Heche, *The Complete Christian Guide to Understanding Homosexuality: A Biblical and Compassionate Response to Same-Sex Attraction* (Eugene, OR: Harvest House Publishers, 2010), p. 466.

2. Kenneth L. Woodward, "Sex, Morality and the Protestant Minister." *Newsweek* 130, no. 4 (July 28, 1997): 62.

3. Eileen Schmitz, *Staying in Bounds: Straight Talk on Boundaries for Effective Ministry* (Danvers, MA: Chalice Press, 2010), p. 114.

4. Tanya Eiserer and Sam Hodges, "Minister at Prestonwood Baptist Charged in Internet Sex Sting." *Dallas Morning News*, May 17, 2008. Retrieved from http://www.bishop-accountability.org/news2008/05_06/2008_05_17 _Eiserer_MinisterAt.htm 2012.

5. State Board of Missions. *Preventing Sexual Misconduct In Your Church*. Montgomery, Alabama: Alabama Baptist Convention, 2012. Retrieved from www.alsborn.org on August 1, 2012.

6. Peter W. Williams, *America's Religions: From Their Origins to the Twenty-first Century* (Chicago: University of Illinois Press, 2008), p. 427.

7. National Center for Victims of Crime, *Child Sex Abuse, 2012*. Retrieved from http://www.ncvc.org/ncvc/main.aspx?dbName=DocumentViewer& DocumentID=32315#9 on June 21, 2012.

8. NPR Staff. "Out of the Closet . . . In the Pulpit of a Mega-church." NPR, November 14, 2010. Retrieved from www.npr.org on June 23, 2012.

9. Omri Elisha, *Moral Ambition: Mobilization and Social Outreach in Evangelical Megachurches (The Anthropology of Christianity)* (Los Angeles: University of California Press, 2011), p. 171.

CHAPTER 7

1. Skye Jethani, "Mega-Churches: When Will the Bubble Burst?" *Huffington Post* (November 8, 2011). Retrieved from http://www.huffingtonpost.com on December 15, 2011.

2. Scott Thumma and Warren Bird, *Not Who You Think They Are: The Real Story of People Who Attend America's Megachurches* (Hartford, CT: Hartford Institute for Religious Research, 2009), p. 3.

3. Dan Harris, "Young Americans Losing Their Religion," ABC News (May 6, 2009). Retrieved from http://abcnews.go.com/Politics/story?id=7513343&page=1 on December 12, 2011.

4. Dan Kimball and Rick Warren, *The Emerging Church: Vintage Christianity for New Generations* (Grand Rapids, MI: Zondervan, 2003), p. 48.

5. Thom S. Rainer and Same S. Rainer, *Essential Church?: Reclaiming a Generation of Dropouts* (Nashville: B&H Publishing Group, 2008), p. 30.

6. Associated Press. "California megachurch Crystal Cathedral gets new name as it changes to Catholic church." *FoxNews.com*, June 10, 2012. Retrieved from http://www.foxnews.com/us/2012/06/10/california-megachurch-crystal-cathedral-gets-new-name-as-it-changes-to-catholic/ on August 1, 2012.

7. Marshall Davis, *More Than a Purpose: An Evangelical Response to Rick Warren and the Megachurch Movement* (Enumclaw, WA: Pleasant Word, 2006), p. 204.

Bibliography

Ahn, Helen Noh, and Gilbert, Neil. "Cultural Diversity and Sexual Abuse Prevention." *Social Services Review*, September 1992.

Alabama Baptist Convention State Board of Missions. *Preventing Sexual Misconduct in Your Church*. Montgomery, AL: Alabama Baptist Convention, 2008.

Associated Press. "Data Shed Light on Child Sexual Abuse by Protestant Clergy." *New York Times*, June 16, 2007, p. A11.

Associated Press. *Secret Service, IRS Investigate Atlanta Megachurch*. FoxNews.com, October 21, 2011. Retrieved from http://www.foxnews.com/us/2011/10/21/secret-service-irs-investigate-atlanta-megachurch/ on November 2, 2011.

Associated Press. "California megachurch Crystal Cathedral gets new name as it changes to Catholic church." *FoxNews.com*, June 10, 2012. Retrieved from http://www.foxnews.com/us/2012/06/10/california-megachurch-crystal-cathedral-gets-new-name-as-it-changes-to-catholic/ on August 1, 2012.

Association of Religion Data Archives (ARDA). *United Methodist Church*. 2012. Retrieved from http://www.thearda.com/Denoms/D_1469.asp on July 3, 2012.

Atlanta Journal-Constitution. "2005 AJC Report: Bishop Eddie Long Benefits from his Own Church's Charity: Between 1997 and 2000, Eddie Long Received $3.07 Million in Compensation." August 28, 2005. Retrieved from www.ajc.com on October 14, 2011.

Baggini, Julian. *Atheism: A Very Short Introduction*. New York: Oxford University Press, 2003.

Bauer, Susan Wise. *The Art of Public Grovel: Sexual Sin and Public Confession in America*. Princeton, NJ: Princeton University Press, 2008.

Benyei, Candace R. *Understanding Clergy Misconduct in Religious Systems: Scapegoating, Family Secrets, and the Abuse of Power.* Binghamton, NY: Haworth Pastoral Press, 1998.

Bilrzikian, Gilbert, and Ortberg, John. *Community 101: Reclaiming the Local Church as Community of Oneness.* Grand Rapids, MI: Zondervan Publishing House, 1997.

Bird, Warren. *Megachurches as Spectator Religion: Using Social Network Theory and Free-rider Theory to Understand the Spiritual Vitality of America's Largest-Attendance Churches.* New York: Fordham University, 2007.

Bishop Accountability. *Sexual Abuse by U.S. Catholic Clergy: Settlements and Monetary Awards in Civil Suits.* Retrieved from http://www.bishop-accountability.org/settlements/ on October 15, 2012.

Bogan, Jesse. "American's Biggest Mega-Churches." *Forbes*, June 26, 2009. Retrieved from http://www.forbes.com/2009/06/26/americas-biggest-mega-churches-business-mega-churches.html on June 23, 2012.

Boys, Don. "Mess in Memphis: Bellevue Baptist, Another Mega-Church in Trouble!" *CSTNews*.com, May 14, 2007. Retrieved from www.CSTNews.com on June 13, 2012.

Brehony, Kathleen A. *Awakening at Midlife.* New York: Riverhead Books, 1996.

Callaway, Michael R., and Esser, James K. "Groupthink: Effects of Cohesiveness and Problem-Solving Procedures on Group Decision Making." *Social Behavior and Personality* 12, no. 2 (1984): 157–164.

Carnes, Patrick J. *Out of the Shadows: Understanding Sexual Addiction.* Center City, MN: Hazelden, 2001.

Center for Ministerial Care. *Ministerial Marriage and Family.* Cleveland, Tennessee, 1998.

Chaves, Mark. *American Religion: Contemporary Trends.* Princeton, NJ: Princeton University Press, 2011.

Chaves, Mark, and Garland, Diana. "The Prevalence of Clergy Sexual Advances toward Adults in Their Congregations." *Journal for the Scientific Study of Religion* 48, no. 4 (2009): 817–824.

Clarke-Stewart, Alison and Brentano, Cornelia. *Divorce: Causes and Consequences (Current Perspectives in Psychology).* New Haven, CT: Yale University Press, 2006.

Cozzens, Donald B. *The Changing Face of the Priesthood: A Reflection on the Priest's Crisis of Soul.* Collegeville, MN: Liturgical Press, 2000.

Dallas, Joe, and Heche, Nancy. *The Complete Christian Guide to Understanding Homosexuality: A Biblical and Compassionate Response to Same-Sex Attraction.* Eugene, OR: Harvest House Publishers, 2010.

Dart, John. "The Trend toward Bigger Churches: Going Mega." *Christian Century* 127, no. 15 (July 27, 2010): 22–27.

Davis, Marshall. *More Than a Purpose: An Evangelical Response to Rick Warren and the Megachurch Movement.* Enumclaw, WA: Pleasant Word, 2006.

Dew, Rachel Elizabeth, Daniel, Stephanie S., Armstrong, Tonya D., Goldston, David B., Triplett, Mary Frances, and Koenig, Harold G. "Religion/Spirituality and Adolescent Psychiatric Symptoms: A Review." *Child Psychiatry & Human Development* 39 (December 1, 2008): 381–398.

Dixon, Thomas. *Science and Religion: A Very Short Introduction*. New York: Oxford University Press, 2008.

Douthat, Ross. *Bad Religion: How We Became a Nation of Heretics*. New York: Free Press, 2012.

Early, Dave. *Pastoral Leadership is . . . How to Shepherd God's People with Passion and Confidence*. Nashville, TN: B&H Publishing Group, 2012.

Einstein, Mara. *Brands of Faith: Marketing Religion in a Commercial Age*. New York: Routledge, 2008.

Eiserer, Tanya, and Hodges, Sam. "Minister at Prestonwood Baptist Charged in Internet Sex Sting." *Dallas Morning News*, May 17, 2008. Retrieved from http://www.dallasnews.com on June 1, 2012.

Elisha, Omri. *Moral Ambition: Mobilization and Social Outreach in Evangelical Megachurches (The Anthropology of Christianity)*. Los Angeles: University of California Press, 2011.

Ellingson, Stephen. *The Megachurch and the Mainline: Remaking Religious Tradition in the Twenty-First Century*. Chicago: University of Chicago Press, 2007.

Eng, James. "Jehovah's Witnesses Ordered to Pay More Than $20 Million to Woman Who Said She Was Sexually Abused." NBC News, June 15, 2012. Retrieved from http://usnews.msnbc.msn.com on June 30, 2012.

Evans-Cowley, Jennifer S. "Good Heavens! Texas Churches Grow to Biblical Proportions." *Commercial Markets*, April 2007. Retrieved from http://recenter.tamu.edu/pdf/1809.pdf on July 4, 2012.

Finch, Susan. "DA says music minister exposed teen to HIV." *The New Orleans Times-Picayune*, August 11, 2000.

Finkelhor, David, Ormrod, Richard, Turner, Heather, and Hamby, Sherry. "School, Police, and Medical Authority Involvement with Children Who Have Experienced Victimization." *Archives: Pediatrics and Adolescent Medicine* 165, no. 1 (January 2011): 9–15.

Finkelhor, David. "Today, Sex Abuse Victims Are Less Alone." CNN, June 20, 2012. Retrieved from http://www.cnn.com/2012/06/20/opinion/finkelhor-sandusky-child-abuse/index.html?hpt=hp_bn7 on July 15, 2012.

Frawley-O'Dea, Mary Gail. *Perversion of Power: Sexual Abuse in the Catholic Church*. Nashville: Vanderbilt University Press, 2007.

Friberg, Nils, and Laaser, Mark R. *Before the Fall: Preventing Pastoral Sexual Abuse*. Collegeville, MN: Order of St. Benedict, 1998.

Goh, Robbie B. H. "Hillsong and 'Mega-Church' Practice: Semiotics, Spatial Logic and the Embodiment of Contemporary Evangelical Protestantism." *Material Religion* 4, no. 3 (November 2008): 284–305.

Grenz, Stanley J., and Bell, Roy D. *Betrayal of Trust: Confronting and Preventing Clergy Sexual Misconduct*. Grand Rapids, MI: Baker Books, 2001.

Griffin, Ricky W. *Management* (2nd ed.). Boston: Houghton Mifflin Company, 1987.

Grosch, William N., and Olsen, David C. "Clergy Burnout: An Integrative Approach." *Journal of Clinical Psychology* 56, no. 5 (2000): 619–632.

Harris, Dan. "Young Americans Losing Their Religion." ABCNews, May 6, 2009. Retrieved from http://abcnews.go.com/Politics/story?id=7513343&page=1 on December 12, 2011.

Helguero, Francis. "Nation's Largest Megachurch Works with Partners to Aid Hurricane Victims." *The Christian Post*, September 16, 2005. Retrieved from www.christianpost.com on September 14, 2012.

Henry, Ryan G., and Miller, Richard B. "Marital Problems Occurring in Midlife: Implications for Couples Therapists." *American Journal of Family Therapy* 32 (2004): 405–417.

Hodges, Sam. "Exclusive: Former employee sues Daystar founder Marcus Lamb over his extramarital affair with another employee." *Dallasnews.com*, December 3, 2010. Retrieved from www.dallasnews.com on June 23, 2012.

Horst, Elizabeth A. *Questions and Answers about Clergy Misconduct*. Collegeville, MN: Order of St. Benedict, 2000.

Hunt, Stephen. *Religion and Everyday Life*. New York: Routledge, 2005.

Internal Revenue Service (IRS). *Tax Guide for Religious Organizations: Benefits and Responsibilities under the Federal Tax Law*. Washington, D.C.: Author, 2012.

Janis, Irving L. *Victims of Groupthink*. New York: Houghton Mifflin, 1972.

Janis, Irving L. *Groupthink: Psychological Studies of Policy Decisions and Fiascoes. Second Edition*. New York: Houghton Mifflin, 1982.

Janis, Irving L., and Mann, Leon. *Decision Making*. New York: Free Press, 1977.

Jethani, Skye. "Mega-Churches: When Will the Bubble Burst?" *Huffington Post*, November 8, 2011. Retrieved from http://www.huffingtonpost.com on December 15, 2011.

Jorstad, Erling. *Popular Religion in America: The Evangelical Voice (Contributions to the Study of Religion)*. Westport, CT: Greenwood Press, 1993.

Jung, Carl G. *Modern Man in Search of a Soul*. New York: Harvest Books, 1933.

Kimball, Dan, and Warren, Rick. *The Emerging Church: Vintage Christianity for New Generations*. Grand Rapids, MI: Zondervan, 2003.

Kohut, A. and Stokes, B. *America against the World*. New York: Henry Holt and Company, 2006.

Kosmin, Barry A., and Keysar, Ariela. *American Religious Identification Survey (ARIS 2008)*. Hartford, CT: Trinity College, March 2009.

Kumar, Anugrah. "Sexperiment: Ed Young Suffers Eye Injury: Leaves Before 24 Hours Over." *The Christian Post*, January 15, 2012. Retrieved from www.christianpost.com on September 14, 2012.

Lammers, Joris, Stapel, Diederik A., and Galinsky, Adam D. "Power Increases Hypocrisy: Moralizing in Reasoning, Immorality in Behavior." *Psychological Science* 21 (2011): 737–744.

Laaser, Mark, and Hopkins, Nancy Myer. *Restoring the Soul of a Church: Healing Congregations Wounded by Clergy Sexual Misconduct.* Collegeville, MN: Order of St. Benedict, 1995.

Laaser, Mark. *Healing the Wounds of Sexual Addiction.* Grand Rapids, MI: Zondervan, 2004.

Lohr, Kathy. "Senator Probes Mega-Churches' Finances." *NPR*, December 4, 2007. Retrieved from www.npr.org on January 3, 2012.

Loveland, Anne C., and Wheeler, Otis B. *From Meetinghouse to Megachurch: A Material and Cultural History.* Columbia: University of Missouri Press, 2003.

Martin, Graham, Bergen, Helen A., Richardson, Angela S., Roeger, Leigh, and Allison, Stephen. "Sexual Abuse and Suicidality: Gender Differences in a Large Community Sample of Adolescents." *Child Abuse & Neglect* 28 (2004): 491–503.

Mastrogiovanni, John L. *Why Ministers Fall: In Search of the Holy Grail.* Seattle: CreateSpace, 2009.

Matthews, Donald H. *Sexual Abuse of Power in the Black Church: Sexual Misconduct in the African American Churches.* Bloomington, IN: WestBow Press, 2012.

McClintock, Karen A. *Preventing Sexual Abuse in Congregations: A Resource for Leaders.* Herndon, VA: Alban Institute, 2004.

McKay, Paul. "Mormons Caught Up in Wave of Pedophile Accusations/Church Deals with Abuse Cases without Reporting Them, Critics Say." *Houston Chronicle*, May 9, 1999, p. 1A. Mental Health America. *Co-dependency.* Alexandria, Virginia: Mental Health America, 2012. Retrieved from http://www.mentalhealthamerica.net/go/codependency on July 6, 2012.

Mock, Brentin. "Bishop Eddie Long." *Intelligence Report* 125 (Spring 2007) Retrieved from http://www.splcenter.org/get-informed/intelligence-report/browse-all-issues/2007/spring/face-right on July 2, 2012.

Moore, Art. "Mega-Church Pastor Resigns, but Denies Sexual Misdeeds." *Christianity Today* 12, no. 8 (July 13, 1998): 26.

Murashko, Alex. "Sex Addiction: Are Pastors More Vulnerable to Sexual Temptation?" *Christian Post*, June 25, 2012. Retrieved from www.christianpost.com on August 6, 2012.

National Center for Victims of Crime. *Child Sex Abuse, 2012.* Retrieved from http://www.ncvc.org/ncvc/main.aspx?dbName=DocumentViewer&DocumentID=32315#9 on June 21, 2012.

National Institute of Justice Journal. "On-the-Job Stress in Policing: Reducing It, Preventing It," January 2000, pp. 18–24.

Neuman, Gary. *The Truth about Cheating: Why Men Stray and What You Can Do to Prevent It.* Hoboken, NJ: Wiley & Sons, 2008.

Niebuhr, Gustav. "Mormons Paying $3 Million to Settle Sex Abuse Case." The New York Times, September 5, 2001. Retrieved from http://www.nytimes.com/2001/09/05/us/mormons-paying-3-million-to-settle-sex-abuse-case.html on October 15, 2012.

NPR Staff. "Out of the Closet . . . In the Pulpit of a Mega-church." NPR, November 14, 2010. Retrieved from www.npr.org on June 23, 2012.

Oakland, Roger. *Faith Undone: The Emerging Church: A New Reformation or an End-Time Deception.* Silverton, OR: Lighthouse Trails Publishing, 2007.

Oleszczuk, Luiza. "Bishop Joseph Walker III Accused of Sexual Assault by 4 Women." *The Christian Post*, March 1, 2012. Retrieved from http://www.christianpost.com/news/bishop-joseph-walker-iii-accused-of-sexual-assault-by-4-women-70631/ on August 1, 2012.

Pepper, Colleen. *Inside the World of Executive Pastors: Leadership Network's 2009 Survey.* Leadership Network, 2009. Retrieved from www.leadnet.org on December 14, 2011.

Pew Forum on Religion and Public Life. *U.S. Religious Landscape Survey (Religious Affiliation: Diverse and Dynamic).* Washington, D.C.: Pew Research Center, February 2008.

Phan, Katherine T. "Bernice King Leaving Eddie Long's Megachurch to Start New Ministry."*The Christian Post*, May 31, 2011. Retrieved from http://www.christianpost.com/news/bernice-king-leaving-eddie-longs-church-to-launch-new-ministry-50707/ on August 3, 2012.

Pinkman, Paul. "Former Jacksonville Pastor Pleads Guilty in Sex Case: Darrell Gilyard Faces 3 Years in Prison, Must Register as Sex Offender." *Florida Times-Union*, May 21, 2009. Retrieved from www.jacksonville.com on August 23, 2012.

Putnam, Robert D., and Feldstein, Lewis. *Better Together: Restoring the American Community.* New York: Simon & Schuster, 2003.

Rainer, Thom S., and Rainer, Same S. *Essential Church?: Reclaiming a Generation of Dropouts.* Nashville: B&H Publishing Group, 2008.

Rasmussen, Dana. *Behind Bars in America, Vol. 3: Federal Prisons in North and South Carolina and Inmates Like Bernie Madoff, Jim Bakker, Mark Whitacre, and More.* Webster's Digital Services, 2011.

Saad, Lydia. "U.S. Confidence in Organized Religion at Low Point." Gallup Politics, July 12, 2012. Retrieved from www.gallup.com on August 2, 2012.

Sanford, John A. *Ministry Burnout.* Louisville, KY, Westminster/John Knox Press, 1982.

Schaller, Lyle E. "Mega-Church!" *Christianity Today* 34, no. 4 (March 5, 1990): 20–24.

Schaller, Lyle E. *The Seven-Day-A-Week Church.* Nashville: Abingdon, 1992.

Schmitz, Eileen. *Staying in Bounds: Straight Talk on Boundaries for Effective Ministry.* Danvers, MA: Chalice Press, 2010.

Shapiro, Nina. "Cash and Carry." *Seattle News Weekly*, February 21, 2007. Retrieved from http://www.seattleweekly.com/2007-02-21/news/cash-and-carry/ on October 10, 2012.

Shelley, Bruce L. *Church History in Plain Language* (3rd ed.). Nashville: Thomas Nelson, 2008.

Southern Baptist Convention. On the Sexual Integrity of Ministers. St. Louis, MO, June 2002. Retrieved from http://www.sbc.net/resolutions/amResolution.asp?ID=1117 on July 4, 2012.

Spellman, Jim. "New Haggard accuser: 'He really thought he was invincible'." *CNN.com*, January 29 2009. Retrieved from http://edition.cnn.com/2009/CRIME/01/28/colorado.church.haggard/index.html on October 14, 2012.

Symonds, William C., Brian Grow and John Cady. "Earthly Empires: How Evangelical Churches Are Booming from the Business Playbook." *BusinessWeek*, May 22, 2005. Retrieved from http://www.businessweek.com/magazine/content/05_21/b3934001_mz001.htm on June 25, 2012.

Thumma, Scott, and Travis, Dave. *Beyond Megachurch Myths: What We Can Learn from America's Largest Churches*. San Francisco: John Wiley & Sons, 2007.

Thumma, Scott, Travis, Dave, and Bird, Warren. *Megachurches Today, 2005*. Retrieved from http://hirr.hartsem.edu/org/faith_mega-churches_research.html#research on September 15, 2011.

Thumma, Scott, and Bird, Warren. *Not Who You Think They Are: The Real Story of People Who Attend America's Megachurches*. Hartford, CT: Hartford Institute for Religious Research, 2009.

Thumma, Scott. *Exploring the Megachurch Phenomena: Their Characteristics and Cultural Context*. Hartford Institute for Religion Research, 2011. Retrieved from http://hirr.hartsem.edu/bookshelf/thumma_article2.html on December 11, 2011.

Turner, Bryan S. (ed.) *The New Blackwell Companion to the Sociology of Religion*. Malden, MA: Blackwell Publishing, 2010.

Twitchell, James B. *Shopping for God: How Christianity Went from In Your Heart to In Your Face*. New York: Simon & Schuster, 2007.

Weber, Max. *Essays in Sociology*. New York: Oxford University Press, 1946.

Weber, Max, and Roth, Guenther. *Economy and Society: An Outline of Interpretive Sociology*. Boston: Beacon Press, 1963.

Wexler, David B. *When Good Men Behave Badly: Change Your Behavior, Change Your Relationship*. Oakland, CA: New Harbinger Publications, 2004.

White, Thomas, and Yeats, John M. *Franchising McChurch: Feeding Our Obsession with Easy Christianity*. Colorado Springs, CO: David C. Cook, 2009.

Wickham, Randall Easton, and West, Janet. *Therapeutic Work with Sexually Abused Children*. Thousand Oaks, CA: Sage Publications, 2002.

Williams, Peter W. *America's Religions: From Their Origins to the Twenty-first Century*. Chicago: University of Illinois Press, 2008.

William C. Symonds, Brian Grow, and John Cady, "Earthly Empires," *Businessweek*, May 23, 2005. Retrieved from http://www.businessweek.com/stories/2005-05-22/earthly-empires on August 5, 2012.

Witherington, Ben. *Looking Haggard, Ted Steps Aside.* November 3, 2006. Retrieved from http://benwitherington.blogspot.com/2006/11/looking-haggard-ted-steps-aside.html on July 3, 2012.

Woodward, Kenneth L. "Sex, Morality and the Protestant Minister." *Newsweek* (July 28, 1997): 62.

Zaimov, Stoyan. "Pastor Darrell Gilyard's Sex Offender Status Divides Fla. Community." *The Christian Post*, February 23, 2012. Retrieved from http://www.christianpost.com/news/pastors-sex-offender-status-divides-fla-community-70039/ on July 25, 2012.

Index

Accountability, lack of, 51–54, 80, 111, 122–23; confidentiality and, 52–53; professional boundaries and, 55; responsibility and, 52; tax-exempt status and, 103–4
Adolescent victims, 40–41, 68, 82–83, 89–90; of Long, 31, 33–34, 50; suicide and, 70
Adultery. *See* Extramarital affairs
Ahn, Helen Noh, 43
Alabama Baptist Convention, 118
America against the World (Kohut & Stokes), 5
American Psychiatric Association, 39
American Religion: Contemporary Trends (Chaves), 110
America's Religions: From Their Origins to the Twenty-First Century (Williams), 9, 120
Anonymity, 33, 73, 74; in mega-churches, 1, 105
Associated Press, 92
Atheism: A Very Short Introduction (Baggini), 109

Atlanta Journal-Constitution (newspaper), 34
Awakening at Midlife (Brehony), 44

Bad Religion: How We Became a Nation of Heretics (Douthat), 2, 100–1
Baggini, Julian, 109
Bakker, Jim, 32, 73, 100
Baptist churches, 52, 80, 82, 89–90; Southern Baptists, 78, 11, 13, 112, 118–19; resolution on sexual abuse, 114–15
Barna, George, 127–28
Barton, Joe, 41
Before the Fall: Preventing Pastoral Sexual Abuse (Friberg & Laaser), 24
Bell, Roy D., 20, 43–44
Benyei, Candace R., 36, 83
Betrayal of Trust: Confronting and Preventing Clergy Sexual Misconduct (Grenz & Bell), 20, 43–44

Better Together: Restoring the American Community (Putnam & Feldstein), 10
Beyond Megachurch Myths (Thumma & Travis), 7
Biblical investigation, 84
Bilrzikian, Gilbert, 4
Bird, Warren, 7, 100
Blaming the victim, 37, 63–64, 67, 84–85; families and, 70; ministers' wives, 95; stigmatization and, 71–72. *See also* Victims, of sexual abuse
Bond, Julian, 50
Boston Globe (newspaper), 120
Branding, 17–18
Brands of Faith: Marketing Religion in a Commercial Age (Einstein), 18
Brehony, Kathleen A., 44
Brentano, Cornelia, 77
Britton, Philip, 82–83
Burnett, Mark, 19
Bush, George W., 19, 33, 105
Businessweek (magazine), 19–20

Carnes, Patrick J., 48
Catholic Church. *See* Roman Catholic Church
Center for Ministerial Care, 58
The Changing Face of the Priesthood: A Reflection on the Priest's Crisis of Soul (Cozzens), 91
Chapel Hill Harvester Church (Atlanta), 31, 55, 80, 120
Charisma, of mega-church leaders, vii, 1, 10–11, 14, 19, 24; abuse of power and, 26, 31, 64; succession and, 129
Chaves, Mark, 62, 110
Cheating, on spouses. *See* Extramarital affairs
Child Abuse & Neglect (study), 70
Child Psychiatry & Human Development (magazine), 109
Child victims, of sexual abuse, viii, 52–53, 63, 67–72, 117; fear of reprisal and, 68; impact on families, 70–71; impacts on well-being, 69; out-of court settlements, 91–92; parental supervision and, 113; Roman Catholic clergy and, 91, 100, 114; sex-offender probation and, 89–90; statistics from studies of, 68–70; training to prevent, 113, 121; vulnerability and, 35. *See also* Adolescent victims
Cho, David Yonggi, 7
Christianity, 101. *See also* Evangelical Christianity; *specific Christian sect*
Christianity Today (magazine), 105, 112
The Christian Post, 50–51
Church History in Plain Language (Shelley), 13
Church of Jesus Christ of Latter-day Saints, 92
Church-state separation, 5, 104–5
Clarke-Stewart, Alison, 77
Clinton, Bill, 49–50
Clohessy, David, 114
Codependency, of ministers' wives, 97–98
Coercion, power and, 26, 27, 29, 30; victims of sexual abuse and, 35, 36, 38, 51
Collective rationalization, 86. *See also* Groupthink, in churches
Community 101: Reclaiming the Local Church as Community of Oneness (Bilrzikian & Ortberg), 4
Community Christian Church, 8
Community movement, 4, 102
The Complete Christian Guide to Understanding Homosexuality (Dallas & Heche), 112
Confidentiality, 52–53. *See also* Silence, of mega-churches
Consumerism, 2, 5, 8, 9
Copeland, Kenneth, 30–31, 106
Coping mechanisms, 45; stress and, 47, 48–49, 123

Index

Cost-benefit analysis, 29
Cozzens, Donald B., 91
Crystal Cathedral, 129
"Cultural Diversity and Sexual Abuse Prevention" (Ahn & Gilbert), 43

Dalberg-Acton, John Emerick Edward, 21
Dallas, Joe, 112
The Dark King (archetype), 23
Dart, John, 7
Davis, Marshall, 129–30
Daystar Television Network, 30–31
Divorce: Causes and Consequences (Clarke-Stewart & Brentano), 77
Dixon, Thomas, 108
Dollar, Creflo, 106
Dominance, abuse of power and, 27–28
Douthat, Ross, 2, 100–101
Drucker, Peter, 101–2
DSM-IV (Diagnostic and Statistical Manual of Mental Disorders), 23–24, 39

Einstein, Mara, 18
Elisha, Omri, 52, 122
Ellingson, Stephen, 3
Emerge Ministries survey, 58
The Emerging Church: Vintage Christianity for a New Generation (Kimball & Warren), 127
Entertainment, in mega-churches, vii, 1, 5–6, 101, 105–6
Essential Church?: Reclaiming a Generation of Dropouts (Rainer & Rainer), 128
Ethics, religion and, 107–8
Evangelical Christianity, 2, 4, 7–8, 33, 55, 65, 122
Exhibitionism, 39
Expert power, 27. *See also* Power, abuse of

Exploring the Megachurch Phenomena: Their Characteristics and Cultural Context (Thumma), 79–80
Extramarital affairs, 30–31, 54, 56–57, 65–66, 112, 120; abuse of power and, 65; guilt and shame in, 74–75; warning signs of infidelity, 94, 95–96

Faith branding, 17–18
The False Lover (archetype), 23
Falwell, Jerry, 32, 105
Feldstein, Lewis, 10
Fetishism, 39, 40
Financial crimes, 66–67, 96–97, 103–4
First Baptist Church of Hammond, Indiana, 80
Fisher, Jeff, 50–51
Forgiveness, ix, 73, 89, 90
Franchising McChurch: Feeling Our Obsession with Easy Christianity (White & Yeats), 5–6
Frawley-O'Dea, Mary Gail, 37
Friberg, Nils, 24
From Meetinghouse to Megachurch: A Material and Cultural History (Loveland & Wheeler), 2, 4
Frotteurism, 39–40

Gaines, Steve, 52, 53
Galinsky, Adam D., 50
Gallup poll, 99–100
Garland, Diana, 62
Gilbert, Neil, 43
Gilyard, Darrell, 89–90
Goh, Robbie B. H., 103
Gorman, Marvin, 73
Greater St. Stephen Baptist Church (New Orleans), 82
Grenz, Stanley J., 20, 43–44
Grosch, William, 46
Groupthink, in churches, 85–88

Groupthink: Psychological Studies of Policy Decisions and Fiascoes (Janis), 86–87
Guilt and shame, 48, 86, 94, 98

Haggard, Ted, viii, 19; male prostitutes and, 33, 54, 55, 73
Hahn, Jessica, 32
Hawkins, Rick, 65–66
Healing the Wounds of Sexual Addiction (Laaser), 25, 42, 48
Heche, Nancy, 112
Hinn, Benny, 106, 107
Homosexual relations, 25, 34, 50, 64, 122; male prostitutes, 33, 54, 55, 73–74; same-sex marriage, 102
Hopkins, Nancy Meyer, 22
Horst, Elizabeth A., 51–52, 83
Hour of Power (television program), 129
Houston Chronicle (newspaper), 92
Hunt, Stephen, 108–9
Hunter, Joel, 19
Hyles, Jack, 80

Ideology, 3, 30, 87–88
Individualism, 2, 3, 99
Infidelity, warning signs of, 94, 95–96. *See also* Extramarital affairs
Inspirational appeal, 27
Instrumental compliance, 27
Insurance claims, 92
Intelligence Report (magazine), 50
Internal Revenue Service (IRS), 80–81

Jakes, T. D., 8, 19, 30, 107
Janis, Irving L., 86–87
Jehovah Witnesses, 91
Jethani, Skye, 125
Job stress, church leaders and, 45–49, 56, 58
Jones, Mike, 73
Jorstad, Erling, 1
Journal for Scientific Study of Religion, 62
Journal of Clinical Psychology, 46
Journal of Pastoral Care, 112
Jumping the Broom (movie), 19
Jung, Carl G., 44

Kemp, Centino, 54
Kimball, Dan, 127–28
King, Bernice, 91, 120
King, Coretta Scott, 50
Kingham, Rick, 64
Kohut, A., 5

Laaser, Mark R., 22–24, 25, 42, 48
Lakewood Church (Houston), 6, 19, 102
Lamb, Marcus, 30–31
Lammers, Joris, 50
Leaders, of mega-churches, 10–12, 17–58, 109–10; abuse of power by, 20–21, 25–38, 56, 82, 91; accountability of, 51–54, 55, 80, 103, 122–23; archetypal descriptions of, 22–24; background checks on, 116–18; as CEO, 79, 81, 116; charisma of, vii, 1, 10–11, 14, 19, 24, 129; coping with job stress, 45–49, 56, 58, 123; corporate branding and, 17–18; denial of wrongdoing, 25; entitlement of, 90–91; financial crimes of, 66–67, 96–97, 103–4; invulnerability of, 86; lavish lifestyles of, viii, 106–7; as "pastorpreneurs," 9; profile of, 17–21; self-confidence of, 28–29, 31, 32; succession of, 128–29; temptation, deception, and accountability of, 49–56; trust and respect for, ix, 11, 110; wives of, 56–58, 93–98. *See also* Marital problems, of church leaders; Sexual misconduct, of church leaders
Leadership (magazine), 112
Legitimate power, 26, 27. *See also* Power, abuse of

Long, Eddie, viii, 81, 119–20; lavish lifestyle of, 107; sexual misconduct of, 31, 34–35, 50, 54, 59–60, 91
Loveland, Anne C., 2, 4

Male power, 20–21. *See also* Power, abuse of
Male prostitutes, 33, 54, 55, 73–74. *See also* Homosexual relations
Marital problems, of church leaders, 56–58, 93–98; divorce and, 76–77; extramarital affairs, 30–31, 54, 56–57, 65, 74, 112, 120; midlife crisis and, 45
Masochism, sexual, 40
Mastrogiovanni, John L., 88–89
Material Religion (magazine), 103
Matthews, Donald H., 82
McClintock, Karen A., 38, 90–91
The Megachurch and the Mainline: Remaking Religious Tradition in the Twenty-First Century (Ellingson), 3
Mega-churches, 107; accountability in, 122–23; anonymity in, 1, 105; array of services offered, 12–13; budgets of, 11, 17; business-driven structure of, 9, 19–20, 81, 103, 113, 115–16; child abuse awareness in, 121; community and, 4, 102, 130; consumerist nature of, 2, 5, 8, 9; corporate branding of, 17–18; decline of organized religion and, 13–14; defined, 6; entertainment focus of, 1, vii, 5–6, 101, 105–6; evangelical Christianity and, 2, 4, 7; future of, 125–31; groupthink in, 85–88; impact on smaller churches, 8, 18; internal investigations in, 84–85, 123; location of, 12; membership profile, 14; nondenominational theology and, 3–4, 8, 13, 80; profile of, 1–15; rise of new ideologies and, 3, 88; Roman Catholic Church compared to, 99, 111, 120, 126; secularism in, 81–82; as "seeker churches," 1, 8, 103; silence of, ix, 44, 52–53, 79–98, 103, 104; small groups within, 10; as sociological phenomena, 101–2; strategies to end sexual misconduct in, 111–24; tax-exempt status of, vii–viii, 80–81, 103–4; youth focus of, 13–14, 106, 128. *See also* Leaders, of mega-churches
"Mega-Churches: When Will the Bubble Burst?" (Jethani), 125
Mellado, Jim, 10, 20
Mental Health America, 97
"Messiah complex," of leaders, 66
Meyer, Joyce, 31, 106
Midlife crisis, 44–45, 57
"Mindguards," groupthink and, 87
Ministry Burnout (Sanford), 46
Moorehead, Bob, 64, 84
Moral Ambition: Mobilization and Social Outreach in Evangelical Megachurches (Elisha), 52, 122
Morality, 86–87, 107–9
More Than a Purpose: An Evangelical Response to Rick Warren and the Megachurch Movement (Davis), 129–30
Mormon Church, 92
Morton, Paul, 82

The Naïve Prince (archetype), 22
National Association of Evangelicals (NAE), 33, 55
National Catholic Risk Retention Group, Inc., 119
National Center for Victims of Crime, 121
National Child Protection Act (1993), 117
National Child Traumatic Stress Network, 67
National Institute of Justice Journal, 47
Neuman, Gary, 56
New Birth Missionary Baptist Church, 31, 34, 81. *See also* Long, Eddie

The New Blackwell Companion to the Sociology of Religion (Turner), 4
New Destiny Church, 54
Newsweek (magazine), 112
Nondenominational theology, 3–4, 8, 13, 80
Nonprofit tax-exempt status, 80, 103, 104

Obama, Michelle, 19
Olson, David C., 46
"On the Sexual Integrity of Ministers" (Southern Baptist Convention), 115
Ortberg, John, 4
Osteen, Joel, 6, 19, 30, 102
Osteen, Victoria, 6, 19
Out of the Shadows: Understanding Sexual Addiction (Carnes), 48
Overlake Christian Church (Redmond, Washington), 64, 84

Paine, Thomas, 108
Paraphilias, 39–41
Parker, Annise, 102
Paulk, Donnie Earl, 55, 120
Paulk, Earl, viii, 31, 55, 120
Pediatrics and Adolescent Medicine (journal), 68
Pedophilia, 40, 92. *See also* Child victims, of sexual abuse
Pepper, Colleen, 11
Perversions of Power: Sexual Abuse in the Catholic Church (Frawley-O'Dea), 37
Pew Forum on Religion and Public Life, 14
Pew Research Center, 107
Popular Religion in America: The Evangelical Voice (Jorstad), 1
Potter's House (Dallas), 8. *See also* Jakes, T. D.
Power, abuse of, 20–21, 25–38, 56, 80; betrayal of trust and, 51, 112–13; charisma of leaders and, 26, 31, 64; child and adolescent victims and, 33–34, 51, 69; church silence and, 82; coercion and, 26, 27, 29, 30, 35, 38; dominance and, 27–28; entitlement and, 90–91; moral hypocrisy and, 50; rational persuasion and, 27, 35; self-confidence and, 28–29, 31, 32; sexual misconduct and, 29–30, 33, 38, 65; sources of, 26–27
Presbyterian churches, 14
Preventing Sexual Abuse in Congregations: A Resource for Leaders (McClintock), 38
"Preventing Sexual Misconduct in Your Church" (Alabama Baptist Convention), 118
Prostitutes, viii; anonymous sex and, 33, 73, 74; male prostitutes, 33, 54, 55, 73–74; mistresses and, 73–77
Protestant religion, 4, 7, 14, 92. *See also specific sect*
Psychological disorders: "messiah complex," 66; mid-life crisis and, 44–45; self-esteem and, 42, 44; sexual addictions and, 38–45; sociocultural factors, 42–43
Psychological effects, of assault, 60–61
Psychological Science (magazine), 28, 50
Psychology Today (magazine), 20–21
PTL (Praise the Lord) Television Network, 32
Putnam, Robert D., 10

Questions and Answers about Clergy Misconduct (Horst), 51, 83

Rainer, Thom S., 128
Rainer, Same S., 128
Rape, Abuse and Incest National Network, 69–70
Rational persuasion, 27, 35
Referent power, 26. *See also* Power, abuse of
Rekers, George Alan, 73–74

Religion: decline in, among young people, 127–28; morality and, 107–9. *See also specific religion*
Religion and Everyday Life (Hunt), 108–9
Religious freedom, 5
Religious ideology, 3, 30, 87–88
Restoring the Soul of a Church (Laaser & Hopkins), 22–24
Reward power, 26. *See also* Power, abuse of
Riggle, Steve, 102
Robbins, Steve C., 65, 66, 109
Roman Catholic Church, viii, 14, 88, 111; distrust of, 2–3; hierarchy in, 99, 126; mega-churches compared to, 99, 111, 120, 126; out-of-court settlements, 91; secrecy and sexual abuse in, 37, 82, 100; SNAP and, 114; VIRTUS programs, 119

Sadism, sexual, 40
Same-sex marriage, 102. *See also* Homosexual relations
Sanford, John A., 46
Schaller, Lyle, 10, 12–13, 105
Schmitz, Eileen, 112
Schuller, Robert H., 129
Science and Religion: A Very Short Introduction (Dixon), 108
Seacoast Church (Mount Pleasant, SC), 9
Second Baptist Church (Houston), 12
Secrecy, 37. *See also* Silence
Secularism, 2, 3, 9–10, 81–82
"Seeker" churches, 1, 8, 103
Self-censorship, 87. *See also* Silence, of mega-churches
Self-esteem, 42, 44, 61, 67, 95, 97
The Self-Serving Martyr (archetype), 22–23
The Seven-Day-a-Week Church (Schaller), 12–13
Sexperiment (Young), 101
Sexual abuse, of children. *See* Child victims of sexual abuse

Sexual Abuse in Congregations: A Resource for Leaders (McClintock), 90–91
Sexual Abuse of Power in the Black Church (Matthews), 82
Sexual harassment, 53, 65, 114; power and, 29–30, 38
Sexual misconduct, of church leaders, 15, 20–24, 50–51; abuse of power and, 29–30, 33, 38, 112–13; extramarital affairs, 30–31, 54, 56–57, 65–66, 95–96, 112, 120; future of mega-churches and, 126–27; internal investigation of, 84–85; lack of accountability and, 51–54, 80; lack of boundaries and, 24–25, 55, 66, 112; leader succession and, 129; midlife crisis issues and, 44–45, 57; ministerial archetypes, 22–24; out-of-court settlements and, 34, 90, 91–92; reasons for, viii–ix; sex-offender probation, 89–90; sexual addictions and, 38–45; sociocultural factors in, 42–43; strategies to end, 111–24, 130; stress and, 48; types of, 39–41. *See also* Child victims, of sexual abuse; Leaders, of mega-churches
Shame, and guilt, 48, 86, 94, 98
Shelley, Bruce L., 13
Shiloh Metropolitan Baptist Church (Jacksonville, Florida), 89–90
Shopping for God: How Christianity Went from In Your Heart to In Your Face (Twitchell), 9
Silence, of mega-churches, 44, 52–53, 79–98; blaming the victim and, 84–85; church image and, 83; forgiveness and, ix, 89, 90; groupthink and, 85–87; ideology and, 87–88; internal investigations and, 84–85; ministers' wives, 93–98; tax-exempt status and, 80–81, 103, 104
Silence, of victims, 34, 37, 43, 64. *See also* Victims, of sexual abuse

Sisyphus complex, 46
Social exchange theory, 29, 77
Social Services Review, 43
Sociocultural factors, 42–43, 109
Solomon, Gordon, 41–42
Southern Baptists, 8, 11, 13, 112, 118–19; resolution on sexual abuse, 114–15
South Korea, mega-churches in, 7
Spirituality, secularism and, 2
Stapel, Diederick A., 50
Staying in Bounds: Straight Talk on Boundaries for Effective Ministry (Schmitz), 112
Stigmatization, 69, 71–72, 83, 91
Stokes, B., 5
Strategies, to end sexual misconduct: accountability and, 122–23; background checks and, 111–24, 116–17
Stress, in mega-church leaders, 45–49; coping mechanisms and, 47, 48–49, 123; marital problems and, 56, 58
Survivors Network of Those Abused by Priests (SNAP), 114
Swaggart, Jimmy, viii, 73, 89, 100
Swilley, Jim, 122

Tax-exempt status, of churches, vii–viii, 80–81, 103–4
Teenage victims. *See* Adolescent victims
Temptation, resisting, 49, 50, 54, 63, 89
Therapeutic Work with Sexually Abused Children (Wickham & West), 69
Thumma, Scott, 7, 79–80, 100
Tims, Zachary, viii, 54
Transvestic fetishism, 40
Travis, Dave, 7
"The Trend toward Bigger Churches: Going Mega" (Dart), 7

The Truth about Cheating: Why Men Stray and What You Can Do to Prevent It (Neuman), 56
Turner, Bryan S., 4
Twitchell, James, 9

Unanimity, illusion of, 87
Understanding Clergy Misconduct in Religious Systems (Benyei), 36, 83
U.S. Religious Landscape Survey, 14

The Very Large Church: New Roles for Leaders (Schaller), 10
Victims, of sexual abuse, ix, 25–26, 32, 35–38, 59–77, 93; adolescent, 31, 33–34, 50, 82–83, 89–90; blaming, 37, 63–64, 70, 71–72, 84–85, 95; coercion and, 35, 36, 38, 51; counseling of, 121, 123; detachment of, 36–37; fear of reprisal and, 63–64, 64, 71, 72, 84; impact on families of, 70–71; Long and, 31, 34–35, 50, 54, 59–60; ministerial archetypes and, 22–24; out-of-court settlements to, 34, 90, 91–92; prostitution and mistresses, 73–77; psychological and physiological effects on, 60–61, 83; sexual addictions and, 41; silence of, 34, 37, 43, 64; statistics about, 62–63; stigmatization of, 69, 71–72, 83; suicide attempts by, 54, 70; vulnerability of, 35, 65. *See also* Child victims, of sexual abuse
Vineyard Church (Columbu, Ohio), 65
VIRTUS programs, 119
Volunteers for Children Act (1998), 117
Voyeurism, 41

Walker, Joseph III, 30
Warren, Rick, 10, 127–28
Watchtower Bible and Tract Society of New York, 91
Weber, Max, 3, 26, 27
West, Janet, 69

Wexler, David B., 45
Wheeler, Otis B., 2, 4
When Good Men Behave Badly: Change Your Behavior, Change Your Relationship (Wexler), 45
White, Paula, 66
White, Randy, 66
White, Thomas, 5–6
Why Ministers Fall: In Search of the Holy Grail (Mastrogiovanni), 88–89
Wickham, Randall Easton, 69
The Wild Card (archetype), 23–24
Williams, Paul, 9, 52, 53, 120
Willow Creek Community Church, 10, 19–20

Witherington, Ben, 55–56
Wives, of church leaders, 56–58, 93–98; codependency and, 97–98; divorce and, 76–77, 98; financial crimes and, 96–97; as "first ladies," 57, 94; mistresses and, 76; warning signs of infidelity and, 94, 95–96. *See also* Marital problems, of church leaders
The Wounded Warrior (archetype), 22
Wuthnow, Robert, 3

Yeats, John M., 5–6
Yoido Full Gospel Church (Seoul, South Korea), 7
Young, Ed, 101

About the Author

GLENN L. STARKS holds a Ph.D. from Virginia Commonwealth University in Public Policy and Administration. He has written several books and articles on government, leadership, and management. He has over 20 years of experience working in the federal government and has taught graduate courses in public administration.

www.ingramcontent.com/pod-product-compliance
Lightning Source LLC
LaVergne TN
LVHW021611100225
803383LV00003B/116